S

u

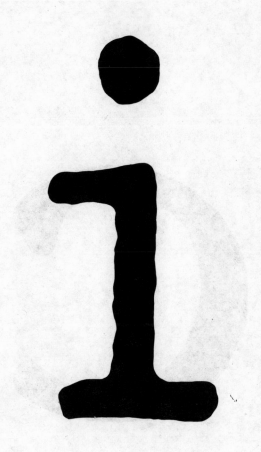

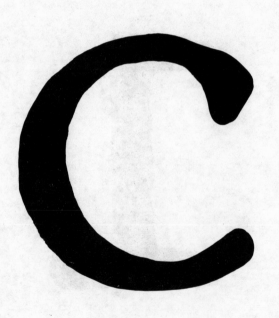

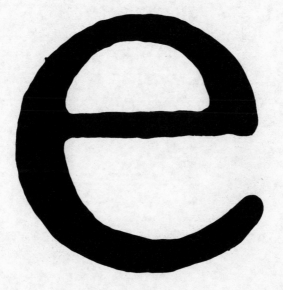

Clyde and Barbara Dodder, General Editors

SUICIDE

PREVENTION,

INTERVENTION,

POSTVENTION

Earl A. Grollman

BEACON PRESS BOSTON

Copyright © 1971 by Earl A. Grollman

Library of Congress catalog card number:
79-141873

International Standard Book Number:
0-8070-2774-X (hardcover)
0-8070-2775-8 (paperback)

Beacon Press books are published under the auspices
of the Unitarian Universalist Association

Published simultaneously in Canada by
Saunders of Toronto, Ltd.

Printed in the United States of America
Second printing, March 1972

CONTENTS

CHAPTER ONE

-- Suicide

The Problem

is a whispered word. How inappropriate for polite
company. Family and friends pretend they do not hear
the dread sound even when uttered. For suicide is a taboo
subject which stigmatizes not only the victim but the
survivors as well.

      Of course, natural death has its share of emotional
overtones: loneliness, disbelief, heartache, and torment.
With self-inflicted death, the emotions are intensified to
unbelievable and unbearable proportions. The person
with suicidal intentions is under intense mental strain
which he feels incapable of resolving. If he succeeds in
taking his life, those left behind experience not only the
pain of separation but aggravated feelings of guilt, shame,
and self-blame. The act of self-destruction raises the
obvious questions, "Why?" and, "What could I have done
to prevent it?" Anxious and grief-stricken, each asks:
"How can I face my friends? What will they think of me?"
Death is a robber. Death by suicide brings the greatest
of all affronts to those who remain. As Shneidman said:

3

The
suicidal
person
places
his
psychological
skeleton
in
the
survivor's
closet.

Until recently, twentieth century man thought of suicide as a private matter. Even many physicians believed that an individual was entitled to die as he wished. To most, self-imposed death was some bizarre form of unconventional behavior, usually signifying insanity. Today, with a greater awareness of the increasing complexity of human life, we must acknowledge that suicide is more than just a personal decision; it is a disease of civilization. The iron curtain of silence has been lifted.

The purpose of this book is both to remove ancient myths and to review the recent studies that have broadened our knowledge of the human dilemma. What can we do for the prevention of suicide, as a clearer understanding before the horrible fact? What can we do for the intervention of suicide, as a helpful communication during the overwhelming crisis? And finally, what can we do for the postvention of suicide, as a meaningful support for those who have experienced the intolerable loss of a loved one through self-inflicted death?

Santayana once said: "That life is worth living is the most necessary of assumptions, and were it not assumed, the most impossible of conclusions."

Suicide Could Happen to You

Almost everybody at one time or another contemplates suicide. Self-destruction is one of many choices open to human beings. Dr. Joost Meerloo, author of Suicide and Mass Suicide, declared, "Eighty per cent of people admit to having 'played' with suicidal ideas." And the medical statistician, Louis I. Dublin, told an aston-

5

ished audience of physicians in Los Angeles: "It would not be rash to estimate that perhaps as many as

2,000,000 individuals are

now living in our country who have a history of at least one unsuccessful attempt at self-execution. A great many of these will try again. On the basis of a recent study, ten per cent will ultimately succeed. I emphasize this fact in order to impress the huge size of the problem with which we are involved and to focus attention on the need for a more concerted effort on the part of socially oriented groups to attack this problem seriously."

No single group, nor race, nor class of people is free from the "unpardonable sin of society." Though one may never utter the word "suicide," does this mean that he is totally free of death wishes? Every person is a potential suicide. Every individual has a tendency to self-murder, which varies in degree of intensity from individual to individual and from one society to another. Bromberg and Schilder found the wish to die frequent in children, and suicidal fantasies common in normal adults. They concluded that the relationship between wishing oneself dead and a suicidal thought or attempt is quantitative rather than qualitative.

The child may think: "If I were to die now, my parents would feel sorry for their meanness." In cases of chronic invalidism, the patient often says: "My affliction is a living death. I would rather die than go on living this way." Or in desperation, the familiar words: I just can't go on any longer," or,

"I
   a
     m

        t
          i
            r
              e
                d

                    o
                      f

                          l
                            i
                              f
                                e,"

                                    or, "My family would
be better off without me," or, "I won't be around much
longer for you to put up with." If these expressions seem
unrelated to suicide, it must be emphasized that these
precise words are the verbal sentiments expressed in
presuicidal communications and conversations.

Threats turn into action. In place of a passive
acceptance of unmanageable difficulties comes an active
declaration of independence — self-imposed death. It
is as if the victim cries out: "At least I am competent to
do this!"

Incidence

Once every minute someone tries to kill himself
with conscious intent. Sixty or seventy times a day these
attempts succeed. Each year in the United States alone,
some reported 25,000 persons take their own lives.

Unquestionably, this number is even higher since
the true cause of death is frequently masked under the
label "accidental." According to the late Dr. Gregory
Zilboorg, Psychiatrist-in-Chief of the United Nations:
"Statistical data on suicide as compiled today deserves

little credence. All too many suicides are not reported as such."

What constitutes suicide in one county, city, or state is often not the same in a neighboring area, and the coroner may be an elected political official and not a physician. Dr. Milton Helpern, Chief Medical Examiner of New York City, says: "In recent years, the inadequacies of most coroner investigations have become increasingly evident."

To many people, suicide is an affront to God, the community, and society, and few experts doubt that many unnatural deaths are covered up. A police chief in a local town admitted, "If a man hangs himself, we just cut him down, rush the dead body to the hospital, and enter some other malady as the cause of death. This way we spare the family the terrible disgrace." THE TRUE AMERICAN SUICIDE RATE MAY BE DOUBLE THE REPORTED ONE!

The problem is worsening. Suicide is the third leading cause of death among young people between fifteen and nineteen years of age. It has been estimated by Yale University School of Medicine that suicide accounts for eight to twelve percent of deaths among college students. The University of Michigan Medical Center reported that cases of attempted and completed suicide seen by its emergency room staff increased eighty-nine percent in five years.

Suicide, which once ranked twenty-second on the list of causes of death in the United States, now rates tenth, and in some states, sixth. Today, the toll is greater than the combined deaths from typhoid fever, dysentery, scarlet fever, diphtheria, whooping cough,

8

meningococcal infections, infantile paralysis, measles, typhus, malaria, bronchitis, and rheumatic fever.

What Is Suicide?

The number of suicides is grossly underreported. Families are loath to have the death pronounced a suicide because of the social stigma attached, as well as the loss of life insurance benefits, since policies do not pay face value under these circumstances. Equally important is the fact that authorities do not always agree as to the means of death.

For example, a young man is found dead with a bullet between his eyes. Beside him is a rifle he has had for a year, with equipment for cleaning it. Accident or suicide?

To be classified a suicide, a person must intend to kill himself and he must actually do so. This is easier said than proved. Did the youth in the above incident intend to take his life? What about the celebrated Marilyn Monroe, with her overdose of sleeping pills — was her intention lethal?

The tool to determine intention is a psychological autopsy. Dr. Edwin S. Schneidman, Chief of the Center for Studies of Suicide Prevention in the National Institute of Mental Health, asserts that a team of social scientists must first interview all the people who were close to the victim and record every reaction and recollection while memories are still fresh. "The investigators would know things about the person that many people close to him did not know about him. And they would find out things about him that he did not know about himself!" The interviewers

9

would then write on the certificate the type of death, using

the abbreviations **N, A, (S,) H**

natural, accidental, suicide, homicide.

Slow Suicide

There are those who are suicidal and yet are not recognized as such. These people find life intolerable and unmanageable and participate in death-oriented behavior. The definition of who and what constitutes a suicide should be expanded to make room for that vast and assorted collection of people engaged in "life-shortening activities." They could well be labeled as either a partial, a subintentioned, a submeditated suicide, or a suicide equivalent.

For people commit suicide without being consciously aware they are doing it. Their entire life-style involves a movement toward the brink of self-destruction. The same psychic forces that impel an individual to jump from the roof of a skyscraper may also be responsible for such dangerous habits as overeating, overworking, or heavy smoking. Sooner or later, many of these subintentioned suicides will succeed in killing themselves. Installment-plan suicides may be less obvious, but are just as deadly.

Autocide

For example, we all know people who constantly drive too fast, cross major arteries against traffic lights, and pass on hills. One place to look out for disguised suicides is on the road. The car serves as an ideal instrument of self-annihilation. The popular wisdom that

10

says, when a car shoots past at ninety, "Man, he's trying
to kill himself," may well be correct.

((AUTOCIDE))

occurs when a vehicle is used as a method of self-imposed
death. Dr. Alfred L. Moseley of the Harvard Medical
School concludes that suicides are a "significant though
unknown" proportion of the 48,000 annual auto deaths in
the United States. And the Federal Center for Studies of
Suicide Prevention, Bethesda, Maryland, claims that
many drivers play latent, unconscious roles in hastening
their own demise. An educated guess is that one quarter
of the drivers who die in auto accidents cause them sub-
intentionally by imprudent and excessive risk-taking.

Rescue, Incorporated, has a number of cases in its
files of people who attempted to kill themselves by "accidentally" smashing their cars into poles, or trees, or
abutments. After studying the personalities and life situations of thirty drivers who died in one-car crashes, Dr.
Robert Litman, of the Los Angeles Suicide Prevention
Center, suggests that about five percent of such accidents
were deliberate. Thus the family of the deceased escapes
the stigma of having a member commit suicide. At the
same time, insurance benefits are promptly paid. It is
for these reasons that persons who attempt autocide
rarely leave suicide notes. The use of the car as a
method of self-destruction is peculiarly resistant to later
observation, statistics, and analysis.

11

Alcoholism

Between one-half and two-thirds of the fifty thousand deaths and two million serious injuries on the highways each year are associated with the excessive consumption of alcohol. In a study at the University of Michigan, Dr. Melvin L. Seltzer examined 72 drivers responsible for automobile accidents claiming 82 lives. He discovered not only that a high proportion of the drivers were alcoholics but that there was a significant relation between accidents, alcohol, and suicidal tendencies. In Maryland, during a five-year period, tests were made for alcohol in the blood in 617 of 1455 suicides, and levels of .05 percent or more were found in 35 percent of the victims. Alcohol deepens aggressiveness, which, when turned against one's self, may lead to suicide.

Alcoholism is a form of life-shortening activity in which a physical disease such as cirrhosis is usually listed as the cause of death. Yet, once again, by drinking to excess the alcoholic plays an unconscious and indirect role in his own demise. He lives in a world of desolation, loneliness, fear, and anxiety. Death is the final release from pain.

Other Forms of Subintentioned Suicide

As usually defined, suicide is the deliberate taking of one's life. It becomes apparent that a larger number of people want to die, but have not reached that state where they will act consciously on a suicidal desire.

Accident-type suicides are not as rare as the casual observer might believe. The accident-prone may believe they are careful, yet they behave in curiously self-

12

destructive ways, such as stabbing themselves with a
knife or "accidentally" taking too many sleeping pills.

A person may not be sure that he wants to die.
Neither is he convinced that he wishes to live. This ambivalence is demonstrated in a deadly "game" called
Russian roulette: By leaving the outcome to external
forces (the place of the bullet in the gun), the decision is
made for him. The gamble with death is also involved in
other daredevil feats, such as auto racing and parachute
jumping.

A suicide equivalent may be camouflaged in idealis-
tic and altruistic garb. The martyr may give up his life

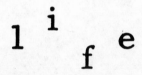

for the honor of God and country for the honor of God and country

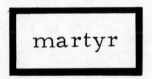

for the honor of God and country. Unconsciously he may
have wished to die. An opportunity presented itself to do
so with honor and nobility. He gains our gratitude, not
our disdain.

These deaths are not ruled as suicides even though
definite unconscious lethal intention is involved. To
clarify the situation, the Suicide Prevention Center of Los
Angeles has proposed three workable psychological

13

classifications for cause of death. An <u>unintended</u> death is one in which an individual plays no active role in his own demise. An <u>intentioned</u> death is one in which the victim has an active part in his own death through deliberate or impulsive acts. In the <u>subintentioned</u> death the victim plays a partial, unconscious, covert role in his own self-destruction.

There are many ways of committing suicide besides slashing one's wrists, or swallowing poison, or shooting or hanging oneself. Suicide, by any name, is the Number One cause of unnecessary deaths. And in the words of Justice Cardoza: "A cry for help is a summons for rescue."

CHAPTER TWO

-- Views on Suicide

Throughout History

People have been killing themselves since the beginning of recorded history. Attitudes toward suicide vary from age to age and from civilization to civilization.

The Roman Stoic who believed that he had had enough of life had his veins severed by trained technicians. The Epicureans considered that one's destiny was a personal choice. Cato, Pliny, and Seneca all found the election of suicide acceptable. However, there were many dissenters. Plato strongly condemned suicidal acts, as did Virgil, Ovid, and Cicero. With the passage of time, although with noticeable exceptions, society began to react in a hostile way against unnatural deaths. Some felt that the manner in which one departs from life reflects not only one's own philosophy of life but a possible contempt for one's group as well. As Kant said:

"Suicide

is an insult

to humanity."

Suicide became taboo. The custom arose of burying
the suicide at the crossroads as a token of disgrace.
Indignities were practiced on the corpse. The body was
dragged through the streets, a stake was driven through
the heart, and the dead person was left for carrion birds
to destroy. Superstitions grew up about the suicide's
ghost. If a pregnant woman stepped upon the grave of a
suicide, it was said, her child would eventually die in a
self-destructive way. Early English practice penalized
the survivors by confiscating their property.

The law dealt with suicide in restrictive terms.
For the legislator who considered suicide as self-murder,
the construct pattern was like this: "Whosoever kills
himself, kills a member of the human genus. He commits
a homicide." Statutes were even enacted against the survivors as a punishment, and as a deterrent for future
offenders.

In England the punishment for an attempted suicide
was imprisonment. Yet, it was discovered, the courts
had no intrinsic ability to prevent the person from taking
his life upon release. Therefore, from 1916, instead of
prison, the individual was placed in the custody of relatives and friends. It was not until 1961 that the British
Parliament enacted a bill abolishing the criminality of
suicide. For the first time in a thousand years the act of
suicide was not considered "A Species of Felony."

In recent years, legal restrictions have been abol-
ished in almost every country. With the rise of research
in mental health, legislation gradually changed. Only in
the United States and India is attempted suicide still an
indictable offense. Today, nine states find suicide

"illegal, constituting a misdemeanor or a felony." But
even in Alabama, Kentucky, New Jersey, North Carolina,
North Dakota, Oklahoma, South Dakota, and Washington
these laws are not scrupulously enforced. Competent
professionals are considered to be of greater therapeutic
value than prison guards to the person intent on taking his
own life. Especially instrumental in the revoking of anti-
suicidal statutes is the stance of religion. For the suicide
laws in the United States were based upon English common
law, which was profoundly influenced by the church and
the synagogue.

Judaism

"And God saw all that He had made, and found it
very good."

With almost the first words of Genesis, a thesis is
stated that has echoed throughout the centuries: life is
good; man should treasure it and never despair of its
possibilities; for behind it is God.

Despite a religious emphasis upon the sanctity of
life, the Hebrew Holy Scriptures contain but six sporadic
references to self-destruction. In each case there are
extenuating circumstances, such as the fear of being
taken captive or the possibility of suffering humiliation or
unbearable pain.

For example, Saul, the first King of Israel (1020
B.C.), was wounded by the Philistines. He called upon
his armor-bearer to slay him in order to prevent his being mocked and tortured by the enemy. Upon the refusal
of the frightened man, Saul fell upon his own sword. In
Flavius Josephus, Antiquities of the Jews, this suicide is

19

condoned as a mark of courage: "And I have a good reason for such a discourse in the person of Saul, king of the Hebrews. For, although he knew what was coming upon him, and that he was to die immediately, by the prediction of the prophet, he determined not to flee from death, nor from love of life to betray his own people to the enemy, nor to bring disgrace on his royal dignity, but exposing himself as well as all his family and children to dangers, he thought it a noble thing to fall together with them, as he was fighting for his subjects, and that it was better that his sons should die thus, showing their courage, than to leave it uncertain what they would be afterwards, for instead of succession and posterity they gained commendation and a lasting name. "

Three references to suicide are found in the Books of Maccabees (165 B. C. – 37 A. D.). Each one relates to martyrdom. When capture by the Romans became inevitable, a Jewish community in 73 A. D. committed mass suicide in the fortress of Massada. Nine hundred and sixty persons killed themselves along this western shore of the Red Sea rather than fall into the hands of the enemy.

In Talmudic times (200– 500 A. D.) an increasing number of suicides is recorded. The rise is partly due to spiritual and social crises, partly to a growing Greco-Roman influence. Now that the act had become more frequent, a condemnatory tone is introduced for the first time. It is stated that the self-homicide forfeits his share in the world-to-come and shall be denied burial honors. The Talmud decrees that a suicide is to receive no eulogy or public mourning. He is to be buried apart, in community cemeteries.

There was never universal agreement. Rabbi Moses ben Nachman, the great Talmudist of the twelfth century, asserted that relatives have a duty to the deceased regardless of the circumstances of death. Other scholars raised important queries concerning suicide: "How do you know that the person really committed suicide, especially if he had not explicity declared his intent nor performed the act in front of witnesses?" "If an individual was found hanging on a tree, could it not have been an accidental death?" "Are the stringent rules valid for minors or the mentally incompetent?"

The sages realized that there were certain extenuating circumstances under which the rigid restrictions and prohibitions could be waived. How can you be certain that a death was truly a suicide? Joseph Caro (1488–1575), perhaps the most outstanding of all the legal authorities, said: "Without proof to the contrary, a man is not pronounced to be wicked. If therefore a man was discovered hanged or choked, as far as possible the act of killing should be regarded as the deed of another person and not as his own deed." What about a minor? "If a minor committed suicide, it is considered that he had done the deed unwittingly." The matter was even approached from the standpoint of mental illness: "If an adult killed himself and it is evident that the act was prompted by madness, he shall be treated as an ordinary deceased person." Although considered a crime against God, suicide could sometimes be explained away, understood, and forgiven.

This enlightened point of view has been incorporated into the approach of the three denominations of modern

Judaism. Rabbi Samuel Korff, Executive Vice-President of the Vaad Harabonim, the Council of Orthodox Rabbis of Massachusetts: "A general review of Halacha [Jewish law] will convince us that a suicidal act cannot be accepted as a 'sane act' under any conditions." Says Rabbi Solomon B. Freehof: "The general custom among Liberal congregations is to bury suicides in their family plots . . . and spare the surviving relatives any disgrace." And Rabbi Max Routtenberg of Rockville Centre, New York: "The [Conservative] Law Committee has generally regarded a suicide as an emotionally distressed and over-wrought person, and therefore not responsible for his actions. It would be almost impossible to ascertain a person's motives and lucidity at the time of such an act. We are inclined to say that he was not in his right mind at that time. He is, therefore, given burial and last rites in the same manner as any other deceased."

In Judaism, suicide may be considered a violation of one of the Ten Commandments. The mystery of God-given life is still the most beautiful gift of all. However, with the growth of the socio-psychological sciences, it is realized that one cannot legislate against self-destruction by religious fiat. Suicide must not be simply condemned. It must be understood and prevented.

Christianity

When Christianity came into being, suicide was very common in Greece and Rome. As mentioned, suicide was even encouraged among the Stoics, the Cynics, the Cyrenaics, and the Epicureans. The early Christians apparently accepted the prevailing attitudes of their era, particularly when persecution made life unbearable. The Apostles did not denounce self-execution; the New Testament touched on the question only indirectly, in the report of Judas' death. For several centuries the leaders of the church did not condemn this widespread practice.

Until Augustine (354–430) denounced suicide as a sin, there was no official church position against it. After deliberating at great length whether self-imposed death could be condoned in the case of a woman whose honor was in danger, Augustine asserted it could not, for "suicide is an act which precluded the possibility of repentance, and it is a form of homicide and thus a violation of the Decalogue Article, 'Thou shalt not kill.'"

The earliest organizational disapproval of suicide was expressed by the Second Council of Orleans in 533. Churches were permitted to receive offerings on behalf of those who were killed in the commission of a crime provided they did not lay violent hands on themselves. Suicide was regarded as the most serious and heinous of all transgressions. In 563 the Fifteenth Canon of the Council of Braga denied the suicide the funeral rites of the Eucharist and the singing of psalms. The Council of Hereford in 673 withheld burial rites to those who died of self-destruction. In 1284, the Synod of Nîmes refused self-murderers even the quiet interment in holy ground.

A further and perhaps more refined elaboration of the Augustinian concept was written by Thomas Aquinas (1224–1274).

23

Aquinas opposed suicide on the basis of three postulates:

1) It was against the natural inclinations of preservation of life and charity toward the self.

2) Suicide was a trespass against the community.

3) It was a trespass against God, who had given man **life.**

For St. Thomas, all life was a preparation for the eternal. His argument therefore stressed the sacredness of human life and absolute submission to God.

The philosophical currents of the seventeenth century brought new views of suicide. At that period of history, religious authority was being questioned and undermined. John Donne, the Dean of St. Paul's Cathedral, was one of the first to start a reaction against the existing

attitudes of the Church toward suicide. He argued that
self-homicide was contrary to the law of self-preservation,
but no more. He viewed it as neither a violation of the
law nor against reason. His position was soon echoed by
many secular writers and philosophers. Hume, Montes-
quieu, Voltaire, and Rousseau wrote essays defending
suicide under certain conditions. They argued for the
greater freedom of the individual against ecclesiastical
authorities.

In modern times, Dietrich Bonhoeffer viewed suicide
as a sin in that it represented a denial of God. "God has
reserved to Himself the right to determine the end of life,
because He alone knows the goal to which it is His will to
lead it." Yet Bonhoeffer suspended this judgment for
prisoners-of-war, who might take their own lives rather
than reveal information that would injure and destroy the
lives of others. The issues of motivation and the greater
good were the significant qualifying tools.

Many Christian groups are not bound to a rigid code
of ethics. A source of change is found in the situation, or
contextual, ethics of Anglican theologians like Joseph
Fletcher and John Robinson. The question of suicide is
an open one that must take into account the particular
situation, the uniqueness of each human relationship, and
the distinctiveness of each person. As Bishop Robinson
suggests: "Truth finds expression in different ages.
Times change and even Christians change with them."

Today, many clergymen not only view the question
of suicide from the theological level, but they also consider the deep psychic causes and also the sociological
implications. Ethical-religious approaches are counter-

balanced with the broader perspectives of the social sciences. Increasingly, suicide is being recognized not only as a religious question but as a major medical problem.

For this reason, groups such as the Anglican Church, taking into consideration modern research, have appointed commissions to revise the harsh religious laws with regard to suicide. The Lutheran Church in America does not regard suicide as an "unforgivable sin," and a Lutheran who takes his own life is not denied a Christian burial.

In the Catholic Church, a directive has been issued to priests in the archdiocese of Boston, relative to Canon 1240 of the Code of Canon Law, which forbids Christian burial to "persons guilty of deliberate suicide." Richard Cardinal Cushing has interpreted the law in this way: "The Church forbids Christian burial to suicides, but only if they were in full possession of their faculties at the time of the crime. The element of notoriety must be present in a suicide for the penalty to be incurred. Hence, no matter how culpable it may have been, if it is not publicly known that the act was fully deliberate, if the culpability is known only to a few discreet people, burial is not to be denied. Ordinarily there is not too great a difficulty in granting Christian burial to a suicide, since most people these days consider the fact of suicide to be a sign of at least temporary insanity." For these reasons, Bishop Thomas J. Riley of St. Peter's Catholic Church in Cambridge has stated that he cannot recall a single recent case in Massachusetts of Christian burial being denied a suicide.

Islam

For Islam, suicide is the gravest sin. In committing suicide one violates his <u>Kismet</u>.

The faithful Moslem awaits his destiny; he does not snatch it from the hands of God.

Suicide is expressly forbidden in the Koran.

Japanese Religious Faiths

Suicide reached its greatest proportions in Japan, where it was embedded in religious and national tradition. Compulsory suicide was a form of punishment granted only to an offender of noble birth. He could expiate his crime and "save face" by dying at his own hands rather than by the sword of the public executioner. Elaborate ceremonies attended this·act. Voluntary hara-kiri was committed for revenge and for other reasons: to protest the policies of a feudal chief or to follow one's lord into the next world. The entire population had been affected by this practice of the noble Samurai, the Japanese warrior caste. Many authorities feel this tradition is still reflected in Japan's suicide rate, until recently the highest in the world.

Critique

Many clergymen still consider suicide to be self-
murder. Reverence for existence and patience in suffering are powerful and profound ethical attitudes that have
ingrained themselves deeply. Hegel reminds us that, "It
is the essence of the Spirit to suffer death and nevertheless to remain alive." Suicide is an action that denies
the value of human life.

But just as jurists have revoked antisuicide statutes,
so have religious leaders reconsidered the concept of
self-destruction. What is accomplished by an ignominious
funeral or by asserting that suicide is a heinous crime
punishable in hell? Says Dr. Stanley F. Yolles, former
director of the National Institute of Mental Health: "Anyone wishing to remove suicide from the sphere of ethics
to treat suicide clinically becomes involved with religious-
philosophical prejudices toward suicide and must overcome them if the suicide program is to be effective."
This religious-moral-social revulsion against suicide
only blocks understanding of what Albert Camus called a

"fatal

game

that

leads

from

lucidity in the face of existence

to

flight

from

light."

No one is suggesting that suicide is desirable or

commendable. But it must be underscored that a species that manipulates nature with nuclear bombs should be less unctuous and more understanding of their fellowman. Instead of thundering pronouncements, the clergyman may better serve by delving into the suicidal person's complex physical and psychological makeup, and then sharing his religious resources of love and understanding. Say the sages: "Do not judge your neighbor until you are in his place."

CHAPTER THREE

-- Suicide

The Theorists

Misinformation and prejudice saturate the complex subject of suicide. Social scientists have therefore dedicated themselves to a clearer knowledge of its psychopathology, which serves as a valuable guide in the detection and understanding of persons with suicidal tendencies. It must be stated at the outset that there is no complete agreement even among the great theoreticians. Each scholar and discipline sheds a different reflection of light.

Sigmund Freud

The "Founder of Psychoanalysis" authored the earliest psychological explanation of suicide. On April 27, 1910, the Vienna Psychoanalytic Society had a discussion on "Suicide in Children." Freud stated that in their zeal to wean children from their early family life, the schools often exposed the immature student too abruptly to the severities of adult life. He said that too little was known about suicide but that perhaps the act was really a repudiation of life because of the craving for death. This remark foreshadowed Freud's later belief in a death instinct.

His paper Mourning and Melancholia presents his theory of suicide. There are two kinds of drives: one is

33

the life instinct, or Eros; the other, the death, destructive, and aggressive drive, or Thanatos. For Dr. Freud,
death is more than a bodily event.

Death is willed.

There is a constant shifting of the balance of power of the
two polar instincts. Eros ages; ageless Thanatos may
assert itself "until it, at length, succeeds in doing the
individual to death."

Thus, suicide and murder are aspects of Thanatos'
impulsive and devastating action. Murder is aggression
turned upon another; suicide is aggression turned upon the
self. Freud's implicit value judgment is that murder is
to be disapproved and prevented because it is highly
destructive. Suicide, too, is murder in the 180th degree
and must also be disapproved and prevented.

Karl Menninger

Dr. Menninger agrees with Freud that there is the
contradiction in life of self-preservation and self-destructiveness. His own close scrutiny of the deeper motives
for suicide posits the hypothesis of three elements.

First, there is the wish to kill. This element is
reflected in the rage of the baby when his desires are
frustrated. "Just as a suckling child resents weaning
and feels that something is taken away from him that it is
his right to possess, so these

34

people who are predominantly infantile cannot stand thwarting."

The wish to kill is turned back upon the person of the "wisher" and carried into effect as suicide.

Another element is the wish to be killed. Just as killing is the extreme form of aggression, so being killed is the extreme form of submission. The demands of conscience are so relentless that there is no inner peace. In order to be punished, people often put themselves in circumstances in which they must suffer. They need to atone by being destroyed.

A final element is the wish to die. This is illustrated in the impulses of daredevil drivers or mountain climbers who want to expose themselves to constant danger. The wish to die is extremely widespread, too, among the mentally ill—the patient believes he will find release from his mental anguish.

Alfred Adler

"To be a human being means to feel inferior." This is fundamental to Alfred Adler's "Individual Psychology." The inability to solve life's problems activates the individual to strive to overcome his inferiority. But some persons, when they fail, need to destroy those around them. Suicide signifies a veiled attack upon others. By an act of self-destruction, the suicide hopes to evoke sympathy for himself and cast reproach upon those responsible for his lack of self-esteem. Adler described the

35

potential suicide as the inferiority-ridden person who "hurts others by dreaming himself into injuries or by administering them to himself."

Carl Jung

Jung stressed the unconscious longing for spiritual rebirth as crucial to a self-imposed death. Not only would one escape the present, intolerable conditions, but by killing himself he could actually hasten the time that he would return to the womb of his mother. He would then become the safe and secure reborn infant. In the picture-language of the symbolized wisdom of the ages ("archetype") is the celebrated Crucifixion—death brings its reward of new life with resurrection.

James Hillman

Perhaps the most forceful defender of the suicide decision is the Jungian analyst James Hillman. He views the preventive approaches of law, medicine, and theology as major stumbling blocks to an adequate understanding of suicide.

Too long, says Hillman, has the view of suicide been colored by moralistic attitudes and the ridiculous idea that it must be prevented at all costs. Medicine has never honestly grappled with the problem since physicians are dedicated to the prolongation of life. The legal tradition has been: We might kill others in many ways and on many grounds without breaking the law; but, hypocritically, we can never under any circumstances justifiably or excusably kill ourselves. And the minister opposes suicide not because the act contradicts God but by "reason" of a fallacious theological dogma.

Hillman believes that suicide is a meaningful and legitimate way of entering death which can "release the most profound fantasies of the human soul."

He quotes David Hume:

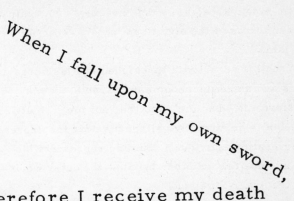

When I fall upon my own sword,

therefore I receive my death

equally from the hands of the Deity

as if it has proceeded from a lion,

a precipice,

or a fever.

Harry Stack Sullivan

Sullivan postulated an interpersonal theory of psychology. Even as electrons are moved by magnetic attractions, so individuals are motivated responsively by other persons who are significant to them. The crucial point is the individual's relationship to other people. He has three personifications of "me." In his security, he

good ↑ me

is the "good me"; in anxiety, he is the "bad me"; in the psychotic nightmares, he is the "not me." He evaluates himself in terms of the significant others' reaction toward him.

When his security is threatened and his unresolved conflicts and anxieties become unbearable, he may wish to transform the "bad me" into the "not me." Self-destruction is an attractive alternative for the depressed, self-deprecating individual. Suicide represents his hostile attitude toward other people—the outer world—redirected against the self.

Karen Horney

Although first trained as a Freudian analyst in Germany, Horney later broke with the classical psycho-analytic movement and rejected Freud's instinct theory. If the infant were given an anxiety-free environment, she said, he would grow and prosper. However, culture, religion, politics, and other similar forces conspire to distort the child's self-development.

The insecure youngster thinks of the world as a hostile place to live. This causes a basic anxiety. Suicide results from childish dependency and from deep-

bad ↓ me

rooted feelings of inferiority, or what Dr. Horney calls
the "idealized image" one has of himself. It may be a
"performance suicide," springing from a sense of failure
in meeting the standards expected by society. To Horney,
suicide results from a combination of personality charac-
teristics and environment.

Emile Durkheim

Horney was not the first to speak about the importance of the social surround. The landmark of sociological research is Emile Durkheim's pioneering effort in

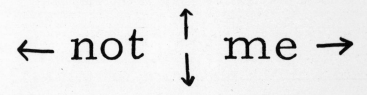

1897, Le Suicide. Durkheim asserted that suicide, which
was then considered a highly individual phenomenon, was
more explicable as a reaction to the peculiarities of society. Incidence of self-destruction could be accurately
traced to the social conditions of the person attempting it.
The degree of suicide is a derivative of that civilization.
Durkheim was successful in tying suicide—the act of one
individual—to the environment in which he lived.

It was Durkheim's theory that there are three types
of suicide. Most suicides are egoistic. The person has
few ties with his community, and there is a relaxation of
religious, family, political, and social controls. Self-
destruction occurs because the individual is not sufficiently
integrated into his society. There is also the anomic

egoistic

(anomie, meaning "lawlessness") suicide, which represents the failure of the person to adjust to social change.
Such suicides may occur in times of business crisis,
like an economic depression; or in an era of prosperity,
suicide may be committed by the nouveau riche who is
unable to adjust to new standards of living.   Lastly is the
altruistic suicide, in which the group's authority over
the individual is so compelling that the individual loses
his own personal identity and wishes to sacrifice his life
for his community.   An example is the soldier who happily
and willingly gives his life for his country.

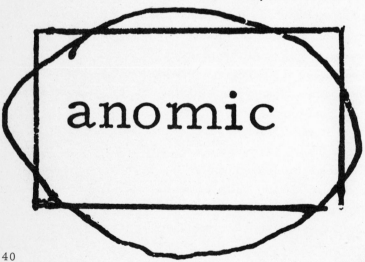

Parenthetically, the sociologists, Andrew F. Henry and James F. Short, Jr., have recently reviewed demographic data to test the Durkheimian hypothesis. The theory still holds up very well. For example, suicide rates are higher in urban than in rural areas. Holding the effects of age and sex constant, the suicide rate for married persons is also much lower than that for single, widowed, or divorced ones.

altruistic

CHAPTER FOUR

-- Suicide

The Social Surround

Emile Durkheim demonstrated how environmental factors are related to the pressures of a life situation. Suicide reflects the relationship of the individual not only to himself but to his community as well.

Self-destruction becomes more understandable when viewed in conjunction with social facts. Suicide rates have a relationship with economic conditions, marital status, age, race, and religion. It must be pointed out that many of the variables may overlap; for example, race with social class. Sociological data may prove inconclusive because valid controls are lacking. Yet, it becomes apparent that society does help to direct the sentiments and activities of the individual towards life or death.

The poet Spenser said it this way:

A foggy mist had covered all the land;
And underneath their feet, all scattered lay

Dead
    souls   and
        bones   of
            men,

Whose
    life had gone
           astray.

Economic Conditions

It has often been said that suicide is the luxury of the wealthy. It is simply not true. For all classes, economic distress brings a sense of hopelessness and despair. Suicide problems are found in blighted areas in ghettos and locations where retired people attempt to subsist on insufficient pensions and welfare programs.

For the very poor as well as for the rich, the rate of suicide soars during periods of economic depression. However, those with the highest status positions react more violently to fluctuations in business. In the period of prosperity of 1920–1923, and again in the depression of 1930–1932, the greatest increase in suicide occurred among the more prosperous. Wealth, the highest token of success, was lost. The affluent's sense of competence was challenged and called into question.

Economic recessions, business reverses, and the loss of employment—all have powerful psychological consequences.

Occupation

The type of job and profession is clearly a factor in suicide. University of Oregon researchers studied self-inflicted deaths in that state for a period of eleven years. They found suicides among doctors, dentists, and lawyers three times as common as among nonprofessional white-collar workers.

According to the American Psychiatric Association, the annual suicide rate among physicians is at least 33 per 100,000, double that of the general white American male population; for psychiatrists, the rate is 70 per 100,000, or four times as great. One-third of these psychiatrists had taken their lives during the earlier years of their professional practice.

Positions of leadership and responsibility may cause unbearable anxieties, especially for the executive of a large corporation. Rapid technological advances may make his skill outmoded if he does not practice continuous self-development. Says Dr. John Post, Medical Director of Zenith Radio Corporation: "The executive's job requires studying at home and his outside activities cut down on family participation." In desperation he may react with sleeplessness, discord with other employees, absenteeism, ulcers, alcoholism, and finally suicide. Instead of fulfillment, there is failure.

Male and Female

Women outnumber men in attempted suicides by a ratio of three to one. For every actual suicide, there may be an estimated eight to ten attempts. The bored housewife is the greatest suicide potential. She makes twice as many attempts as all other female classifications. Rescue, Incorporated believes that a majority of such housewives are crying out for help because the home, the proverbial center of family life, has become a virtual prison. The woman's needs as an individual are not satisfied; her life is not fulfilled.

Even though attempted suicides are higher among women, completed suicides are higher among men. For actual suicides, the percentage of male and female are seventy and thirty respectively. Do men kill themselves with greater frequency because of their more intimate involvement with the competition of the external world, while women are closer to the more secure inner world of home and children? Or are men more skilled with lethal weapons like guns and thus more able to "successfully" complete the task of self-annihilation?

It is known that men most often commit suicide by shooting or hanging. Women almost always use passive means of self-destruction: sleeping pills, poisons, or gas. They prefer not to shed their blood or disfigure their bodies.

Marital Status

Students of epidemiology have consistently reported
that suicide is less frequent among married persons.
There is one noticeable exception—the young married
population. While marriage is generally considered a
buffer against self-inflicted death, the rate of suicide
under age twenty-four is much higher for married than
for single persons. This reversal is most dramatic for
those under the age of twenty, teen-agers who may have
rushed into an ill-advised marriage to escape an unsatis-
factory home environment or been forced into a wedding
because of pregnancy. From age twenty-four, the odds
favor the married individual. This unusual pattern is
rarely discussed, although Durkheim reported back in the
nineteenth century that early marriage had an "aggravating
influence on suicide."

The suicide rate to the age of thirty-five is higher
for the widowed than for the single person. Problems
facing the young widow are especially severe. The death
of the family breadwinner often comes at a time when she
and her husband were actively engaged in raising a family
and paying the mortgage on their home. Death shatters
not only the emotional life of the survivor but abruptly
leaves her to cope with difficult family responsibilities
alone.

From the age of thirty-five, the rate of suicide of
the single person is higher than that of those who have
experienced the death of a spouse. Her children play an
important part in helping the widow feel needed. The
young give her a purpose for existence. In contrast, the
single person may feel adrift without a caring family. The

future suggests only more loneliness and alienation.

Divorced men and women have a higher suicide rate than the undivorced of the same sex. The world of the divorced person is society's

never-never land.

It is fraught with emotional problems of social isolation, guilt, bitterness, and hostility.

Age

The frequency of suicide increases with age. Below the age of fifteen, suicides are extremely rare. The curve then rises sharply from 3.6 per 100,000 in the 15-19 group, to one of 27.9 per 100,000 in the 75-84 age bracket. Two-thirds of male suicides and more than half of the female suicides are over forty-five years of age.

Children

Suicide is rare among children. For ages five to fifteen, there has been little variation over the years, either by race or by sex, with a rate of approximately 0.2 per 100,000.

When suicide is accomplished, it often relates to masturbation. The child's physical gratification is diminished by his secret guilt and shame. For in the mythology of his civilization, the act is labeled a sign of moral depravity which brings insanity and imbecility. The sensitive youngster is in conflict between his sexual needs and the rigid judgments and pronouncements of his church and family, as well as the misinformation from his elders. Death may be a way out of the terrifying dishonor and self-degradation.

Youth

"I remember my youth and the feeling that will
never come back anymore—the feeling that I could last
forever, outlast the sea, the earth, and all men." So
rhapsodized Joseph Conrad.

Many young people today would disagree. Suicide
ranks fourth as the cause of death among the general adolescent population. From ages fifteen to nineteen the
suicide rate is 5.5 per 100,000 for boys and 2 per

100,000 for girls. Among college
students, suicide has
become the second most
frequent cause of
death, surpassed only
by accidents. The count goes up
when one realizes that some students kill themselves in
what are called "accidents."

For every 10,000 college students, says Dr. Dana
L. Farnsworth, Director of the Harvard University Health
Services, 1,000 will have emotional conflicts severe

enough to need professional help; 300–400 will have feelings of depression deep enough to impair their efficiency; 100–200 will be apathetic and unable to organize themselves; 20–50 will be seriously affected by conflicts within the family; 15–25 will need treatment in a mental hospital; 5–20 students will attempt suicide; 1 to 3 will succeed.

Why? "Pressures starting from early childhood are the one important motivation of suicide," states the American Orthopsychiatric Association. "Attempts of young people to end their lives are based on depressed feelings of being rejected, abandoned, and unable to meet competition."

A terrifying concern of the student is his inability to compete successfully in school. Failure brings not only disappointment and disapproval from his parents but a shattering of his own personal confidence. Those who knew the suicide victim often use these words: "he pushed himself too hard," "worried over grades," "felt his marks were not as good as they should be." In short, scholastic anxiety triggers the suicidal crisis.

One youth wrote this suicide note to his parents: "You've hounded me about grades to the point where I can't even study. You keep telling me that I'll never make it. So I'm doomed to failure—and you've made me feel that failure is the worst thing that can happen. My mid-years last week were a nightmare. I can't shake this terrible depression that has come over me. The only thing left for me is this bottle of sleeping pills."

Many of the young people have difficulties with interpersonal relationships. Some of those who

contemplate suicide have been involved with a stormy love
affair. Now that the romance is broken there is more than
just disappointment. There is the tumultuous feeling of
being rejected and abandoned. This is tantamount to the
complete loss of self-esteem. Loss of love precipitating
loss of life, which is seen frequently in real life, is af-
firmed in literature (Shakespeare's Romeo and Juliet and
Goethe's Werther) and in many popular and classical songs.

Others have gone to college and never really made
friends. They are described as being "reserved" or
"shy." But there is no one really to rap with, to confide
in. They are alienated from the most minimal social
interactions. Long ago, they lost communication with
their parents. They compensate for their personal loneliness by increased study and almost total absorption in
school work. But learning is no substitute for companionship. A most calamitous example of human isolation is
the student who was found in his room after he had been
dead for eighteen days. What a tragic commentary on his
existence! There were no friends, no one involved enough
in his life to know or to care that he had been missing for
more than two weeks.

College health workers are alarmed over the increased number of suicide attempters in their student
populations. Counseling services are sorely needed to
help the young people. Yet only seventy-six colleges
offer therapy in campus clinics by professional psychologists and psychiatrists.

The university itself must reevaluate its position in
the life of the youth. College should be more than an ex-
tension of a dreary, regulation-bound high school and

53

more than a model of the great "rat race" in which young people pursue grades and not human growth. The institution of higher learning should assist in the challenging task of the second decade of life, in which the youth must determine who he is, and what he wants to be, to find identity and self-fulfillment.

Middle Age

The young person looks forward to the years when at last he will be settled. Then the torment of the scholastic life and the anticipation of military service will be over. His home will be established and he will be well along in his chosen business or profession. Yet, statistical tables demonstrate a rise in the frequency of suicide during the middle years.

Graying hairs and deepening lines are sharp reminders of life's relentless forward march. No longer does the middle-aged person move so easily and quickly. He often feels weary and is concerned that he does not sleep so well. Jokingly, he declares: "I am not what I used to be." Actually, it is not really funny. He realizes that he is growing older and people his age actually do die.

Along with physiological alteration is psychological change. His hopes have not been realized and are in fact now perceived as unrealizable. His goals have not been attained and are in fact now perceived as unattainable. There are the endless marital and familial conflicts with spouse and children. Suddenly the revelation: "What good is it all? All I have ahead of me is more failure and defeat."

Especially among executives and professionals, a

new term has been coined. It is called "flameout," or the
mid-life crisis. In general terms, the pattern goes like
this: A rising young executive, aflame with creative ideas,
moves through a series of regular promotions. Then in
what should be highly productive middle years, he suddenly "flames out."

f
 l
  a
   m
    e
      out

Dr. Herbert Klemme, Director of the Division of
Industrial Mental Health at the Menninger Foundation,
explains: "As a person reaches the crest of life, after
age thirty-five or so, he begins to struggle with the inevi-
tability of his own death. He has to revise his life goals
in terms of what it is still possible to do. He has to be
realistic and settle for a little less than he had hoped to
achieve. For the person who is not reaching the goals he
has set for himself, the effects can be unsettling or even
devastating."

In business and finance there is a tremendous emphasis on youth. A survey of the presidents of 471 of the
largest companies in the United States showed that the
average age of assuming the firm's top position dropped
from 54 in 1962 to 49 in 1967. "Flameout" is a way out
for one who sees his youthful creative drive slipping away
and for whom aspiration has become frustration.

56

So suicides increase during the middle years. Statistics indicate that in one 12-month period there were 1,400 suicides of Americans ages 30 through 34; 1,800 in the 35 through 39 age bracket; more than 2,000 in the 40 through 44, and in the 45 through 49 brackets; and more than 2,200 among Americans aged 50 through 54.

The Elderly

The poet Robert Browning said in his poem Rabbi Ben Ezra: "Grow old along with me!
        The best is yet to be,
        The last of life, for which the first was made."
People await their senior years. Age is supposed to bring peace to troubled souls.

Yet, the suicide problem is at its highest among elderly citizens. It is in the seventies and eighties that the peak danger exists for both male and female. Elderly persons who choose suicide are really serious about ending their lives.

Year in and year out, the older people rank at the bottom of the list for suicide threats and attempts. Annually, they top the statistics of those whose suicide has been completed.

57

Many of the aged feel out of place in today's society. Emphasis is upon "young ideas." At age sixty-five they are summarily dismissed from productive occupations. For some, it is not only a discharge from a job but from life. No longer do they feel integrated in their community. No longer do they feel useful, valued, and needed.

Degenerative disease sets in. The elderly are prone to the arteriosclerotic states of arthritis, respiratory ailments, and heart disease. Many have serious defects in vision and hearing. Some are confined to bed during their final years, limited to four walls and no companionship. Ill health is a major cause of suicide among the elderly.

It is little wonder that, with loneliness, lack of integration, acute physical pain, and financial insecurity, many elderly persons suffer mental breakdowns. A recent British study of suicide among the aged reveals that one-half of the cases investigated had psychic disorders. There were chronic feelings of discouragement, loss of general competence, and a major shift of self-image. Being physically and mentally incapacitated, they contemplate self-destruction as a solution to the inevitable.

Ingredients vital to the morale of people of all ages— love, caring, and understanding—are so often forgotten when elderly people are concerned.

Cities and Neighborhood

Partly due to the concentration of elderly people, the suicide curve ascends in a westerly direction and is highest in the mountain and Pacific states. Two Florida cities, Miami and St. Petersburg, with a large number of aged and invalided people, also have a high suicide ratio, about twice the national average.

Obviously, there are reasons for suicide other than age. Nevada, for example, has an extremely high rate due to gambling losses and a large transient population. The personally unhappy, the occupationally dissatisfied, the seekers after Nirvana go not only to Nevada but to California to seek contentment.

San Francisco borders on the Pacific Ocean; there is an abrupt limitation to further westward movement. Many people, chasing their particular "pot of gold" by following Horace Greeley's advice, find they have the same difficulties when they have reached the "limit." Suicide seems the only way out. San Francisco is also the national leader in alcohol consumption, another factor in making that city the nation's suicide capital, with a rate two and a half times that of the nation as a whole. Los Angeles also has a strikingly high rate. Hopes are not always achieved in glamorous cities. For unrequited dreams, self-inflicted death becomes a "last resort."

The suicide rate falls steadily from its high point in cities of over 100,000 population to its low point in rural areas. This is attributed to the complex psychological aggravations of city life. The model suicide committer and attempter in Los Angeles County lives in an apartment or an apartment-house area. In the constant mobility, the individual lacks social organization, roots, and a sense of belonging.

Many southern cities, such as Chattanooga and Knoxville, Tennessee; Corpus Christi, Texas; and Greensboro, North Carolina, boast low suicide rates, mainly

because they are peopled by a goodly proportion of Negroes, who in the South rarely kill themselves.

Race

The black people who live in the rural areas of the
South seldom take their lives. Generally, southern
whites are twice as likely to kill themselves as Negroes.
The statistics change drastically in the northern cities.
In a preliminary to a broad Harlem study, Dr. Herbert
Hendin states that among black males age 20 to 25, the
suicide rate runs twice as high as for New York white
men of the same age. After 35 the Negro rate levels off,
while the white rate goes up sharply. Having survived
the "concrete jungle," the black male is no longer
tempted to die in it.

When Negroes migrate to northern industrial centers, the rate of suicide rises markedly. The difficulty
the individual experiences in integrating himself into a
different society, a step for which he is not always adequately equipped, leads to egoistic self-destruction. He
also becomes more prone to anomic suicide because of
the higher self-expectations and problems in economic
adjustment attendant upon a closer relationship with the
white community.

Most of the research to date has been concerned
with members of the white and black races. Only recently has Dr. Harry L. Dizmany investigated the American Indian. He discovered a virtual suicide epidemic
among those between the ages of 15 and 20.

"The Indian adolescent," Dr. Dizmany stated, "not
only experiences a constant struggle to derive an individual

60

identity from a highly disrupted family setting, but also
faces the problem of acquiring a social identity from a
disorganized culture. He is caught, in fact, between two
cultures: one for which he is unprepared, the other which
he feels has failed him and toward which he has a deep
ambivalence. He is neither an Indian, with a sense of
pride and respect for his people and his culture, nor an
assimilated outsider able to identify with the culture and
traditions of the dominant group. In his adolescence, the
Indian youth thus begins to

experience a diffusion of identity and the psychologic chaos of not knowing who he really is or even why he has a right to exist.

Suicide then often becomes, paradoxically, the only way
the Indian boy can have any sense of control over his own
destiny. "

Country

One striking feature of statistics on suicide is the
wide disparity between countries. Most of the high suicide nations are industrialized and urbanized. The United
States, for example, has an average of 11 persons per
100,000 who take their own lives. In Ireland it is 2.5.
And Nicaragua has the least of all the nations.

Latest figures from the World Health Organization show West Berlin to have the greatest incidence of suicide: 58 male deaths and 33 female deaths per 100,000 residents. Brothers are so close and yet so far. A wall divides West Berliners from their loved ones in East Berlin.

The ten nations in which the suicide problem has been the greatest during the twentieth century are, in this order: Austria, Switzerland, Germany, Denmark, Japan, France, Sweden, Belgium, Luxembourg, and the United States. Obviously missing is the rate of suicide in Russia. The Soviet Union does not publish such statistics because suicide is "a bourgeois solution to life's problems."

It is difficult to isolate the variables that determine the prevalence of suicide in one country and its absence nearby. The late President Eisenhower once associated suicide with the welfare states of Sweden (18.5 per 100,000) and Denmark (19 per 100,000). But Norway is also a highly socialized land, and has a lower rate (7.9 per 100,000) than the United States. Also, the high rates in Denmark go back a century or more, predating the welfare state. If anything, the current rate shows a modest decline.

bellycutting

No longer is Japan the most suicidal nation in the world. When that country is mentioned, many immediately think of shinju, the love pact suicide, and hara-kiri, which means "belly cutting." But mandatory hara-kiri has been outlawed for almost a hundred years. And Japan's suicide

rate (16.1 per 100,000) is only slightly higher than that of
the United States.

War

In order to evaluate the suicide rate of a nation, one
must first define the internal conditions that exist at a
particular time. For instance, it has long been determined that there is a significant suicide reduction among
citizens of all age brackets during a national war.

A study of pre-war, war, and post-war suicide
rates in ten countries indicates that in every case, self-
imposed death was less frequent from 1915 to 1918 and
more frequent again from 1926 to 1930. War is usually a
time of patriotism, of social integration, of national purpose. Each citizen—male and female, white, black, and
yellow, old and young—is needed for the great effort of
victory. It is a time of hope not only for military success
but for a better world for all mankind. With an increase
in purpose, there is a decrease in suicide.

Also, through war, people find an honorable way to
vent their aggressions, and for this they are even re-
warded with medals and accolades. In Freud's words:

"The willingness to fight may
depend upon a variety of
motives which may be lofty,
frankly outspoken, or

unmentionable. The pleasure
in aggression and destruction
is certainly one of these. The
death instinct would destroy
the individual were it not
turned upon objects rather
than the self, so that the
individual saves his own life
by destroying something
external to it."

Time of Year

More suicides occur in the spring, when one's deso-
late feelings are confronted by the bloom and burgeoning
of nature. The bleakness of winter seems to match one's
unhappiness, but there is a great contrast between the
bright days of spring and the dark self. Historically,
spring neuroses are identified with the old seed-sowing
festivals and the provocative accompaniment of wine,
women, and song. The sharp dichotomy between the
smiling spring world and a despairing state of mind is one

of the factors in determining the act of one's self-imposed
death. As the poet T. S. Eliot said, "April is the cruelest
month." The April suicide rate is the highest for any
month, and is some 120 percent above the average for the
rest of the year.

During the Christmas period there is also a high
rate of suicide. Depressed by broken homes, death, loneliness, business and social failures, people find that they
are not achieving the joy they expect during the "happy
season." Sorrowfully, they resort to taking their own
life. A study by the Arthur P. Noyes Institute for Neuro-
Psychiatric Research reveals that in December New
Hampshire has its highest number of suicides, and also a
sharp rise in admissions to mental hospitals.

Some consider the act of suicide a quest for rebirth.
Pastoral Psychology devoted an entire issue to "Christmas
and Suicide." A psychiatrist analyzed how some of his
patients identified themselves with the baby Jesus and how
the Saviour died that the faithful might live. Christmas is
part of a "holiday" syndrome, distinguished by a desire
for a new birth like Jesus and a magical resolution of the
unsettled problems of life.

Religious Affiliation

According to Emile Durkheim, religious affiliation
is an important factor in determining whether one will die
of natural or unnatural causes.

The project co-director of the Los Angeles Suicide
Prevention Center, Dr. Norman Farberow, believes that
the suicide rate for Jews is lower than the national average. "The Jews are too interested in life, production,

and creativity for suicide." For the Jew to value his life so little as to destroy it, is in a sense to identify with those who devalued the lives of his martyred ancestors. In addition, there are strong family ties that give him a cohesive relationship to kin and community.

The highest suicide rate is generally considered to be among the multi-factioned and loosely federated Protestants.

Durkheim asserted that, like the Jews, the Catholics have a lesser incidence of suicide. The church brings an integration into men's lives with its tightly knit church order and its authoritarian body of common beliefs and dogmas, including the belief that suicide is a mortal sin, punishable in the life hereafter.

But do Catholics really have a lower suicide rate? It is difficult to be sure. Catholic and Protestant Ireland, for example, both have the same low suicide tolls, and Catholic Austria's rate is the highest of this century.

Today, the ghetto walls have crumpled and those religious and ethnic differences that separated peoples are gradually disappearing. Religious statistics are dif-

How do we recognize the suicidal person? How do we recognize

ficult to compile. In California, the death certificate
does not indicate religion. Compilation of data is woe-
fully incomplete. Even the word Jew, or Protestant, or
Catholic is deceiving and deceptive. Is he a practicing
Jew? Does the Catholic attend Mass? Is the word Protestant a mark of commitment or a facile title implying
"Miscellany"?

The point is self-evident: On the basis of the statistical study of the relationship between suicide and religious
affiliation, simple deductions cannot be effectively tabu-
lated as a single-dimensional technique. Just as different
religions judge suicide differently, so there are variations
of attitudes and sociological changes even within the same
faith over a period of time. Clearly, the suicide rate is
influenced by many factors besides the religion of its
population, i. e., economic conditions, social traditions,
degree of urbanization, and the prevailing political climate. But even more important than statistics is the
most crucial problem of al: "How do we recognize the
suicidal person? "

the suicidal person? How do we recognize the suicidal person?

CHAPTER FIVE

-- Clues to Suicide

Prevention

"Why did he use his power and intelligence to destroy that power and intelligence?" This is the question asked by almost everyone who knew the suicide victim.

Sociologists explain self-destruction in terms of the barometer of social tensions. Psychologists interpret it as a response to the various levels of personal pressure. All agree that suicide occurs when there appears to be no available path that will lead to a tolerable existence.

But not everyone who is cut loose from community ties or faces a business failure becomes a suicide. There is no single reason why a person takes his life. There are only multiple factors that differ from individual to individual.

"But if only I had known that he was thinking of taking his life," the survivors bewail. "I had no indication that such a terrible thing might happen."

Yet, almost everyone who thinks about self-imposed death gives some

clues

to his intended action. Suicide does not occur suddenly, or impulsively, or unpredictably, or inevitably. It is the final step of a progressive failure of adaptation.

Of would-be suicides, eighty percent indicate their intentions in one way or another. Sometimes it is a subtle intimation; often, the threat is unmistakably direct. Significantly, three-fourths of those who have taken their life had made visits to their physician on one pretext or another within four months of the act. It was almost as if they were seeking an opportunity to speak out and to be heard. Too often both professionals and family just do not listen.

A suicidal episode occurs in the form of a crisis of limited duration. The person has ambivalent feelings. He may experience hopelessness but at the same time hopes to be rescued. Often the factors for and against suicide are so evenly balanced that if those close to him would respond in a warm, concerned, and knowing way, the scales could be tipped in favor of life. This is why it is so important to be aware of the clues and warnings which are communicated by the suicidal person.

The Suicide Attempt

The surest sign of intent is the attempt. There is no more dramatic and poignant cry for help. Too often people will dismiss the incident with the exasperated comment: "He was only trying to get attention."

Any suicide effort must be taken with the greatest seriousness.

Twelve percent of those who attempt suicide will make a second try and succeed within two years.

Four out of five persons who do kill themselves have attempted to do so at least one time previously. After an abortive try, many resolve: "I'll do a better job the next time." And they mean it.

The Suicide Threat

Another danger signal is a person's talking of taking his life. The verbal threat should also be viewed with the utmost concern.

The old myth that "those who talk suicide are merely talking and will never do it" has proved dangerously false. To the contrary, many people who have taken their lives had spoken about it, and in so doing, disclosed their inclinations. Initially, the threat could be an unconscious appeal for protection and intervention. Later, if no one is really concerned, the person may set the time and determine the method for the self-execution.

Some suicidal persons are less clear in their communication of intention. Clues are veiled and disguised. Statements such as "You would be better off without me" or "Life has lost all its meaning" may be indications that the person is beginning to formulate plans for his own demise.

The play Quiet Cries emphasizes the verbal hints uttered by suicidal characters: "I want to cut out." "I

won't be here much longer." "Take care of my husband."
"I won't be needing anything." "I won't be here." "I want
out." "I'm going away on a long trip." "I have nothing to
live for." "I won't be around any more." "There won't be

a next week." **"I'll be away."**

Sometimes the coded indications are nonverbal.
The member of a church abruptly resigns under the guise
of moving to another location. The parsimonious man
suddenly makes outright, generous grants of cash to relatives and friends. The youth gives away all his valued
books and prized phonograph records. Once a person has
decided to kill himself he almost always acts a little bit
differently.

The Situational Hint

Prodromal clues may be physical attempts, verbal
threats, and behavioral aberrations. Often the intimation
is situational. Something is happening both <u>within</u> the
person and <u>around</u> him. For suicide often occurs
when status is destroyed or shaken. An individual plays
many roles, and may change some of its parts without
major trauma. However, in a crisis situation his whole
personal ideology is threatened and exposed. He is so
embroiled in this extremity that he loses all perspective
and balance. A person may kill himself because he is
driven by guilt of the past, or he may kill himself because
he cannot accept the alarming prospects of his future.

In San Francisco, the situational findings of suicide
are representative of the United States. These are the
commonest precipitating factors, in order of frequency:

First, there is <u>poor health</u>. A long and painful sickness is always difficult to bear. Persons who take their own lives often envisage leaving behind, in the memories of others, an image of themselves as they were—vigorous, salubrious, and hearty. It has been suggested that Ernest Hemingway chose to die with a "symbolic statue" of himself as a brave, masculine, and virile person rather than to live out his days as a weak, sick old man. Especially in dealing with the chronically ill, one should be especially alert to the variety of forms of suicidal communication.

<u>Economic distress</u> affects more than just the pocketbook. Of course there is the crucial problem of food, clothing, and shelter. But in addition the competence of the person is called into question. He feels that he is a failure and has made a botch of his life. His future is suddenly uncertain, and self-annihilation is contemplated as a way out of the situational dilemma.

With the death of a loved one, life will never be the same. The familiar design of family life is disrupted. The potential suicide may have an unusually long and severe grief reaction. There may be a continued denial of reality even many months after the funeral, or a prolonged bodily distress, or a persistent panic, or an extended guilt, or an unceasing idealization of the deceased, or an enduring apathy, or a sustained hostile reaction to both friends and family.

He cannot face the loneliness and the void in his life.

He may expedite death as a relief from his psychic pain, or as a way to be united with his loved one, or even as a punishment for imagined or real acts perpetrated against the now deceased.

In many ways, <u>divorce</u> and <u>domestic difficulties</u> are more difficult to handle than death. When a person has died, there is the physiological explanation: "He had cancer." Or the theological approach: "The Lord giveth, the Lord taketh away." With divorce, physical and religious reasonings are of no avail. Particularly where youngsters are involved, there are the practical questions of custody and support, along with unconscious feelings of guilt, failure, and revenge. Domestic problems have a profound effect on both parent and child. Studies reveal that many people who eventually kill themselves are the products of a broken home.

Specific stressful situations, such as illness, economic distress, death, and domestic difficulties, often overwhelm a person's defenses. Despair and helplessness result from life's crisis. The situational hint is conducive to a suicidal response.

The Family Hint

To understand the suicidal person, one must be aware of the circumstances of his family. Often he mirrors their emotional disturbances. The environmental situation could determine whether his potential for self-destruction becomes activated.

For example, an individual is disquieted and perturbed. But he is not the only one. The other members of the household may also be in the throes of despair. In a study of adolescents who had taken their lives, it was discovered that almost all of the victims' mothers were themselves depressed and preoccupied with suicide.

Or the rest of the family might be inflamed with anger and resentment. To vent their spleen, they unconsciously select one member to become the object of their accumulated aggression. Unfortunately, he does not know how to cope with their

malice. He cannot retaliate
and respond appropriately.
When he finally decides to
take his life, he is really
acting out the antisocial
impulses that are covertly
present in the other family
members.

There may be a crisis situation—death, divorce, or loss of employment. The family's reaction to this change is one of wild alarm. Someone must pay for the disruption of social relations. The most vulnerable is the family member who is the least belligerent and articulate. Over and over, the "scapegoat" is told that he is the "bad one" who is responsible for the "terrible mess." He is even held chargeable for the death of a person who died of natural causes. By taking his life, he may sincerely believe that he is protecting those whom he loves the most. As a matter of fact, the suicidogenic family may even believe that by the bizarre behavior of self-execution the real problem of the household is now solved.

Suicide cannot be meaningfully studied unless related to the social setting of the person involved. The needs,

78

goals, and strivings of the significant others must be taken into account. One must understand the emotional climate of the family before he can understand the individual member.

Emotional Hint

Emotional symptoms provide some of the best clues to a possible suicidal danger. Any sudden change in a person's personality is always a perilous warning.

The majority of potential suicides suffer from depression. Depression usually begins insidiously, with feelings of apprehension and despondency. A person may not even remember when it all began. All he knows is that lately he has been feeling sad, blue, "down-in-the-dumps." The future looks bleak and he thinks that there is no way he can change it. He imagines that he has cancer, insanity, or some other dread malady. As a matter of fact, he has been thinking a lot lately about death and dying.

lassitude

Ordinary tasks become difficult to perform. "I just can't concentrate and think clearly," he complains. He has difficulty in making even the simplest kind of decision. There is a lassitude and lack of energy. He is always so tired.

A signal of depression and associated suicidal thoughts may be the falling off of sexual activity. The disturbed person may think that he is sterile or impotent.

Intercourse is not pleasurable anymore. Dr. Norman Tabachnick is convinced that sexual complaints may be the calling card of those bent on self-destruction. Investigation of such complaints may reveal a depressive condition which, on deeper probing, may prove to have suicidal concomitants. Sexuality represents a protection against suicide when it is part of a pleasant and satisfying total relationship with another person. It is part of the intimacy and closeness of a meaningful interpersonal experience.

Physical complaints are frequent among suicidally depressed people. Severe insomnia, with early morning awakening (4, 5, or 6 A.M.) and inability to get back to sleep, poor appetite, dry mouth, constipation, and considerable weight loss can occur singly or in combination. Headache, back pain, palpitations, and blurred vision may also be experienced.

In his social functioning, the depressed person prefers more and more to be alone. He loses interest in previously enjoyed activities. The preoccupation with himself usually is in a negative, self-reproachful, and self-deprecating way. When he does talk, he may express a certain inner shame and guilt. But he speaks less frequently, because he has a deep-seated antagonism toward those normally near and dear to him. He neglects his personal hygiene and appearance. There is a marked decline in his job performance.

Of course, not everyone reacts in the same way. There are those who do not look depressed. They may even state how happy they are. They never, never complain. Through thick and thin, they bear immense inner burdens, taking pride in garnering praise for never whimpering, blaming anyone, or shedding a tear. "How well she took her husband's death," one says; or, "Nothing ever gets him down." So clandestinely do some keep their troubles and their feelings about them, that if such a person destroys himself, everyone is astonished and cannot imagine the cause. Actually, one reason is this very secrecy. It is easier to share a burden than to carry it alone.

Beware, too, of depressed people who recover suddenly, without obvious reason, and who assume a calm and settled purposefulness. Often it is the calm before the storm—and their purpose:

the decision to die.

Mental Illness

It is difficult to define "mental illness" and "mental health." Definitions vary from social scientist to social scientist and from discipline to discipline. One approach is that of the Los Angeles Suicide Prevention Center, which describes mental illness as "functional changes in which there is less achievement than usual of life-preserving and other valuable goals." The crux of the concept is that as a result of a new overwhelming responsibility, the organism loses some of its ability to judge and organize. The Center believes that mental illness leads to self-destruction by interfering with life-preserving patterns.

To be mentally ill does not mean to be psychotic. The great majority of suicides are in touch with reality, can care for themselves, and on the basis of their symp-

toms are not committable to a mental hospital. At the
time of the act, they may be desperate. But so are many
"normal" people who do not take their lives.

Among those who are psychotic (estimated at less
than one quarter of suicidal patients), the rate among
schizophrenics and manic-depressives is disproportion-
ately high. Psychotically depressed people often become
suicides either when entering or leaving a totally depressed
state. When encapsulated within it, they are often too
immobilized to kill themselves.

Those Most Susceptible to Self-Destruction

These are the clues to people with the greatest
suicide predisposition:

- Previous suicide attempt

- Suicide threat—direct or disguised

- Chronic illness or isolation

- Bereavement

- Financial stress—bankruptcy, joblessness

- Domestic difficulties—divorce, separation, broken home

- Severe depression

- Psychosis—withdrawal, confusion, depersonalization

- Alcoholism—drinking uncontrolled for a period of
  eight years

- Chronic use of bromides, barbiturates, or hallucino-
  genic agents

- Family history of suicide

A composite picture of a suicidal person:

- Male sex

- Caucasian race

- Adolescent, or over 40 years of age

- Unemployed, retired, or with recent trouble

- Widowed or divorced

- Living alone

- Previous suicide attempt

- Delusions of somatic disease

- Troublesome somatic disease

Caveat emptor: Let the professionals as well as the family and friends beware of oversimplification or jumping to conclusions. Because a person possesses one—or even more—of these symptoms is no conclusive indication that he is suicidal. At the same time, all must be aware that a combination of distress signals manifested over a considerable period must bear watching. After the helping person has detected a cry for help, he must understandingly and lovingly administer first aid to the potential suicide.

CHAPTER SIX

-- Helping the Potential Suicide

Intervention

Fortunately, no one is 100 percent suicidal. Notes often reveal the following kind of mingled emotions: "Dear Blanche, I have to kill myself. I hate you. All my love, Ed." Since the most ardent death wish is ambivalent, suicide is more preventable than any other cause of death.

Attitude of Helper

Suicide is ugly for onlookers, devastating for relatives, and harrowing even for those professionally involved. So the entire subject is often studiously avoided, even when a person threatens to take his own life. Some just do not want to become entangled in the sordid predicament.

Disinterest, however, is not the same as neutrality. To the contrary, the aloof and unfeeling attitude is communicated to the highly sensitive, troubled person. It only confirms his suspicion that no one truly cares.

The Helper as Moralizer

Because of ancient religious and historical taboos, numerous people regard the suicidal person with bias and bigotry. So when the threat is made, "I'm going to do away with myself," their response is, "You can't do that! It's against God and the faith."

The potential suicide is
already suffering from a
heavy burden of punishing
guilt feelings. One who
speaks about suicide as an
immoral act will not only
block the possibility of further
communication, but may
actually contribute and
advance the individual's
present sense of discouragement and depression. For
the suicidal person, self-
destruction is not a theological
issue; it is the result of
unbearable emotional stress.
88

The Angry Helper

Everyone is a suicide potential. Any reference to self-annihilation may expose the listener's own repressed thoughts and impulses. That is why the person who threatens to kill himself often intimidates those who surround him. They resent the suicide-confronter because he reminds them of their own unresolved conflicts.

Since the individual with suicidal tendencies is overwhelmed by sadness, discouragement, and disillusionment, he may act in a hostile manner. Unfortunately his family and friends often react with a reciprocal indignation. They resort to seething emotional arguments which only provoke the disgruntled individual to an even greater fury. They are more concerned with the depressed person's infantile behavior than with meeting his desperation on a more caring and supportive level. By losing their cool, they may lose a life.

Forming a Relationship

There are no cut-and-dried answers to the profound problem of suicide. But the helper can take a giant step forward by demonstrating an unshakable attitude of acceptance toward the perturbed person. Much depends on this quality of relationship. It should not be one only of words, but a nonverbal communication of empathy; this is not the moment of moralizing, but for loving support.

Instead of chastisement, the disquieted person should be put at ease and made to feel understood. To one who feels unworthy and unloved, caring and concern are great sources of encouragement. Thus, the helper is more likely to pierce the harassed individual's prison of isolation.

The Art of Listening

Working with a depressed person who is bent on self-destruction is an awesome responsibility. How frightening to realize that one wrong word might cause another individual's death! Yet, psychotherapists have long recognized the value of listening more and talking less. For when a person has a

disgust of life,

he needs desperately to ventilate his burdensome feelings. This means that those who are concerned could be of invaluable assistance by responsive listening, by giving full attention to what the distraught person is saying and feeling. When hidden thoughts are able to come to the light of day, troubles may seem less complicated and more solvable. The anxiety-ridden individual may even think: "I don't know the solution. But now that I have brought my difficulties out in the open, maybe there is some slight hope, after all."

Professional and nonprofessional alike should cultivate the art of "listening with a third ear." This means to concentrate not only on what is said, even between the lines, but on the nonverbal manifestations: how a person acts, his appetite, his changing moods and outlook, his agitated motor behavior, his irregular sleep pattern, and his impulsiveness in the face of an acute situational problem. These major precursors to suicide are often communicated in various deceptive ways and might be detected by the perceptive listener.

The Art of Communicating

There are channels of communication besides reflective listening. The despondent person may need verbal advice because he cannot entirely choose his own route. He is in

severe psychic pain

and does not always think logically. All he knows is that life is black and death is the only answer.

The first task in crisis intervention is to identify the source of the distress. This may be difficult since suicide thrives on secrecy. Relevant questions, to stimulate discussion, are: "What has been happening to you lately?" "When did you begin to feel worse?" "What is new in your life situation?" "What persons have been involved?" The potential suicide should be encouraged to diagnose the problem in his own words and to pin down as precisely as possible the precipitating stresses.

The troubled individual should be assured that he can express his true feelings with impunity. This includes the negative emotions of hostility, hate, anxiety, grief, resentment, bitterness, and even a desire for revenge. To piously assert: "How could you dare think and say such a thing?" is only to turn him off from future discussion. If he is reluctant to share his innermost emotions, his affective responses might be expedited by observations: "You seem to be quite sad." "You appear to be ready to cry." Or a statement:

"You seem so troubled. Perhaps if you told me how you feel, I might understand."

The present emergency may be a disintegrating relationship with spouse and children. It may be unresolved grief. There may be an organic disease. Keep the feelings and troubles in view.

Once the crisis is more clearly identified and the venting of emotions has taken place, the next step is to clarify how the person has handled similar situations prior to this time. The process is referred to as making an "inventory of problem-solving resources." One listens for references to experiences in the person's past which are analogous to the current scene. He might be asked: "Does this remind you of the way you have felt before?" Together, a determination may be made of the coping methods which had previously worked and may be useful now.

Try to discover what still matters to him. What does he still value? Watch for signs of animation when the "best things" are touched on (noting especially his eyes). What is still available that has meaning? Who are those persons that continue to touch his life? Now that his life's situation is reexamined, are there no alternative solutions? Is there not some ray of hope?

Hope

Hope moves a person out of suicidal preoccupation.
Evidence is demonstrated in the behavior of the Jews during the spectre of Hitler's concerted effort of annihilation.
In the last few years before 1940, the average number of
suicides in Holland for the month of May was 71.2. In
May, 1940, immediately after the Nazi invasion there
were 371. People took their own lives in anticipation of
being sent to the dreaded concentration camps.

Initially the Jews who were interned retained some
kind of faith in victory, with the confidence that families
would soon be reunited. There were relatively few suicides in the camps as long as a shred of hope remained.
When the conflict came to seem endless and news of the
German slaughter of millions reached the inmates, the
number of suicides grew to epidemic proportions. Still
another wave took place at the end of the war when the
former inmates discovered that their loved ones were
dead and the full appalling horror of their death camp
experience was realized.

Many suicide notes reveal the loss of hope and the
seeming impossibility of a meaningful future. Self-
destruction follows when the person no longer has any
measure of optimism and when this sense of futility is
somehow confirmed by those close to him. Someone once
said: "We make fun out of people who hope and we put
people in hospitals who do not."

Hope, however, must be based on reality factors.
It is of little avail to banter the cliché: "Don't worry,
everything will be all right," when everything will not be
all right.

93

Hope springs not from fantasy but from the capacity both to wish and to achieve.

A person who has died cannot be brought back to life, no matter how much one hopes and prays. Yet the survivors may discover some new meaning in life, even though it will never be the same again. If a ship goes on the rocks there is a difference between hoping to swim to the near shore and hoping to reach the other side of the water.

When someone loses all hope for any kind of meaningful future, he may need the booster shot of having someone suggest alternatives. He should be able to eventually discover that not everything is monolithic and one-sided.

Of course, since he suffers inner distress, everything looks totally bleak. But he need not be fixated on one end of a polarity. He can love without denying his

honest hate at times; life can
still have some purpose even
in pain. Darkness and light,
joy and sorrow, success and
suffering — all of these are
indispensable strands in the
texture of existence.

The element of a realistic hope must be communicated in
an honest, convincing, and gentle manner.

Help

A message of optimism is relayed that life can be
better than the despair which is currently being experienced. Frequently this is exactly what the discouraged
person is seeking. For just as he contemplates death as
a solution, he seeks a reassurance for life.

Once the source of distress is identified, the counselee has a greater insight into the nature and reality of
his self-destructiveness. He begins to recognize the real
nature of the crisis and his accompanying emotions. He
is made aware of memories which had long been repressed,
or aggressions which he had never before recognized, or
consequences which he had failed to anticipate. With the
possibility of options, feelings of guilt and fear of reject-
tion can be minimized. Maybe there is hope after all.

This does not mean that the potential suicide always responds with tenderness and acceptance. One minute he may be hostile and belligerent. A moment later his mood shifts and he becomes friendly and appreciative. Once again the person intent on killing himself is ambivalent. In words, he may say: "Leave me alone. I don't want you." In action, he may demonstrate that he desperately wants and needs help.

The Family as Helper

A sense of isolation is dangerous for the depressed person. That is why the cooperation of the family should in many cases be enlisted.

Very often relatives might give information that had been "accidentally" overlooked by the troubled person. In this way the pieces of the psychological jigsaw puzzle are more aptly put together.

For alongside Sigmund Freud's will-to-pleasure, Alfred Adler's will-to-power, and Viktor Frankl's will-to-meaning, is another, more basic human striving—the will to relate. It is the quality of a man's association with his family that may determine his ability to withstand the crisis situation.

Unfortunately, it may be that no one really cares if the person does take his life. Sometimes a suicide represents the fulfillment of a subtle and unspoken wish of others. The hidden attitudes of

96

the family have to be gauged with as much care as those of the potential suicide. Occasionally, the beneficiaries even anticipate cashing in an insurance policy. More often, the suicidal person may be an alcoholic, an embarrassment, a general nuisance. One may even ask himself, were he this individual's spouse, or his father, or his son—would he really want him alive? Families are not always helpful. To the contrary, unconscious efforts may be on foot to rid the world of this "terrible" person.

The Church and Synagogue

Susceptibility to suicide is lowest among those who have strong community ties. Involvement in church or synagogue groups may help the disquieted person feel that he is part of a religious fellowship bound together by ties of sympathy, love, and mutual concern. Houses of worship often substitute for a missing family.

The clergyman might pose spiritual alternatives to the counselee's ultimate anxieties, i. e. , death, guilt, suffering, and failure. In relieving the terrible burden of guilt, the pastor could be most effective in his role as the surrogate of the God of Forgiveness. He has unusual power to modify an overstrict conscience and permit the individual a more normal and bearable range of human living.

Support by a network of meaningful relations may mean the difference between coping or collapsing under pressure.

The Professional

The suicidal person has a limited focus, a kind of "tunnel vision." His mind does not always present him with the complete picture of how to handle his intolerable problems. His first requirement may be his need for help to get help. Friends may mean well but they may lack expertise and experience, besides being emotionally involved.

Already mentioned as a possible helper is the clergyman. William James thought of suicide as a "religious disease," the cure for which is "religious faith." Many ministers are superb pastoral counselors—understanding, sensitive, and supportive. But there are others who are completely untrained in crisis intervention. By moralizing with pious platitudes, they may push the parishioner into further isolation and self-recrimination.

Whenever in doubt, the family physician is a fine resource. He usually knows the intimate background of the patient and would be most helpful in both evaluation and referrals. Meanwhile, he might suggest some effective antidepressant drug to tide the person over until help is forthcoming.

The helpfulness of the psychiatrist or clinical psychologist should never be underestimated. And, contrary to popular belief, mental health care is not just the luxury of the affluent. There are private as well as public agencies, supported by national, state, and county funds, which offer a wide range of services at low cost. By his acquired basic knowledge, skills, and attitudes, a therapist has a disciplined capacity to understand an individual's innermost feelings, demands, and expectations. The

98

disquieted person is able to reveal his deepest anguish and fearsome burdens in the sanctuary of a psychotherapeutic consultation.

Constructive planning is discussed with the client to the end that tension and discomfort may be lessened. Environmental changes might be contemplated; suicidal

dis qui et ed

tendencies remain acute until there are desirable alterations in one's life. Hopefully, the mood of self-destruction can be replaced with understanding and the challenge of growth.

It does not always work this way. If the family situation seems weak, or if for any reason the physician feels uncomfortable or concerned about the patient's safety, hospitalization in a psychiatric facility may be the only alternative. Delay at this point can be dangerous. Hospitalization often proves to be a relief to both the patient and the family. It is, however, no panacea. Suicide may occur when the person is allowed to go home from the institution on leave, or shortly after discharge.

A recent study was undertaken by Miller and Godman entitled "Predicting Post-Release Risk Among Hospitalized Suicide Attempters." A most significant factor was the attempter's definition of his situation at the institution. Did he consider the hospital a school where he was a pupil, or a prison where he was incarcerated?

Those who defined the mental hospital negatively at the time of admission and of release were the highest suicide risks.

Another consideration was the manner in which the hospitalized considered their life situation. Those most prone to self-destruction viewed their crises in specific, personalized terms, rather than as a general, diffuse state of change. They reacted to perceived problems with violent, angry thoughts against their "significant others," later turning their fury against themselves as partial retaliation. They viewed their family as "negative others" because of a continued communication blockage.

Investigation continued following their release from the hospital. The above-mentioned high risk cases made poor social adjustments in the community. Some did in fact take their lives; others reattempted and were again institutionalized.

With Continuing Care

Once the initial emergency is past, no one—professional or family—can relax completely. The worst may not be over. Improvement is often confused with the person's increase of psychomotor energy.

Just prior to suicide, many depressed people rush into a welter of activity. They contritely apologize to anyone whom they think they offended. Too often the friends breathe a sigh of relief and let down their guard. This phase may reflect only an inner resolve to wipe the slate clean. Now they can do away with themselves. And indeed, half the individuals who do commit suicide do so within ninety days after the precipitating crisis.

100

Helping a person and his family through a suicidal situation is a difficult and exhausting task. The close relatives must learn to cope and adjust to such feelings as shame, guilt, and anger.

Sometimes forgotten in the tumult is the individual who attempted to take his life. Ironically enough, many regard the person who attempts suicide and survives as a failure. He earns the double contempt of being so deranged that he wanted to die and so incompetent that he couldn't even do the job properly. There is difficulty in finding acceptance both in his family and in the community.

The emotional problems which led to the suicidal crisis are seldom fully resolved even when the extremity has seemingly passed. The emergency is not over until the would-be suicide is at home with life.

To this end, suicide prevention centers have been established for both research and prevention.

The Suicide Prevention Center

There are organizations for muscular dystrophy, multiple sclerosis, epilepsy, cerebral palsy. Yet, until recently efforts to control the major problem of suicide have been negligible. After all, does not an individual who _wants_ to kill himself have a _right_ do do so?

But studies in the last decade now demonstrate that people want to kill themselves for only a relatively brief period of their lives. The suicide prevention center was established to afford the potential suicide an effective sanctuary until the destructive impulse had passed. This pioneering social institution affords the disquieted person a place to turn to when all else seems lost. Help is forthcoming.

Past History

In 1774, in England, the Royal Humane Society was created to frustrate attempted suicides. One hundred and thirty-three years later, in 1907, the National Save-A-Life League was established in New York City, staffed by sensitive nonprofessionals who were seriously concerned about the problem. In 1958 two clinical psychologists, Drs. Edwin S. Schneidman and Norman L. Farberow, formed the Suicide Prevention Center of Los Angeles, one of the most effective and sophisticated of resources, whose competent personnel include psychiatrists, psychologists, social workers, plus a large number of carefully selected volunteers. Over 26,000 people have sought help from the Center.

In Boston Father Kenneth B. Murphy organized Rescue, Incorporated, in 1959. The agency, located at the Boston City Hospital, utilizes the volunteer services of seventy clergymen and also the help of medical professionals. In a five-year period, Rescue, Incorporated, received 7, 893 calls from the depressed, the chronically ill, the alcoholic, and the lonely. All who sought help were answered. Hundreds were rescued in the gravest hour of personal need.

Today there are over 130 suicide prevention centers in operation, including Seattle's Crisis Clinic, Suicides Anonymous in Johannesburg, South Africa, and the Anti-Suicide Department of the Salvation Army in London. In Miami, in order to contact the Suicide Prevention Volunteers one simply dials

F- R- I- E- N- D-S.

Present Function

"What can you do for a person on skid row or should he just die?" This is a transcript of an actual telephone call, part of a long-playing record for use in training suicide prevention workers. The caller is desperately searching for some way out of the trap of his own logic, which has brought him to the conclusion that the only choice is between skid row or death.

Each communication is taken seriously. At the Los Angeles Center, fully ninety-nine percent of those who seek help are sincere; thirty-three percent of the callers are depressed but not to the point of imminent self-destruction; ten percent are moderately to seriously in danger; and from one to six percent are people who, at that very moment, are on the verge of taking their life.

The worker must first evaluate the lethality of the call—the strength of the caller's drive to kill himself. If the person is standing at the telephone with a gun in his hand, then obviously immediate help is needed. The "significant other"—parent, child, lover, friend—might be notified of the situation and, if possible, be involved in the lifesaving efforts.

The telephone therapist attempts to reduce the lethality, so that when the call is ended the distressed person is less likely to end his life. "Many people who threaten suicide just want somebody to talk with," says Henry Warren, President of National Save-A-Life. He believes that his organization, with its telephone counseling and referrals, saves a thousand lives a year.

Once the immediate crisis is over, the person may be referred to the proper social service or psychiatric helper.

Workers are not only helpful at the telephone. They might be prepared to be of assistance at the place where death is threatened.

Rescue, Incorporated, finds that the clergyman may be helpful during the moment of crisis. Occasionally the appearance of a loved one will also cause the person with suicidal preoccupation to reconsider.

When great heights are involved, as when a person threatens to jump from a building or a bridge, the helper might divert attention by offering a cigarette, or a drink, or a message in order to bring the subject to within reach of rescue. A circular ground net may also be erected.

Once the person steps

               off

                    into

                        space

                            there is no
turning back. So every degree of teamwork is exercised
by the suicide prevention center, the professional staff,
the significant others, the clergy, the police, the firemen
to the end that life can be saved and preserved.

Future Service in the Community

Since one of the purposes of the center is to reduce
suicide, research is vital. Much needed data is carefully
collected and analyzed. Together with universities and
clinics, the center works toward a more comprehensive
interdisciplinary understanding. For example, Harvard
University, Boston College, Boston University, and Boston City Hospital teams evaluate the cases handled by
Rescue, Incorporated, in an effort to pinpoint such aspects of the suicide problem as cause, method, and effective means of prevention.

Educational material is distributed to physicians,
nurses, hospital personnel, police, judges, and clergymen so they may be alerted to the clues of the presuicidal
person. Public information is disseminated to help overcome the popular prejudices and mythologies concerning
those bent on self-destruction.

For the individual who threatens or attempts to kill
himself the suicide prevention center extends lifesaving
assistance, compassion, and support.

And finally, when all else has failed, there is help

105

for the "living victims"—the survivors who bear the
burden of guilt and the stigma of having had a loved one
who has willfully taken his life.

CHAPTER SEVEN

-- When a Suicide is Committed

Postvention

The cry for help goes unheeded. A person kills himself.
Life is over.

For the family, tragedy is
just beginning. There is just
not enough time to heal the
wounds of a self-inflicted
death. The crushing blow is
a bitter experience for all
those left behind. They
carry it in their hearts for
the rest of their lives.

The death of a loved one is devastating. Yet the
bereaved may find consolation in believing that it was

God's will, or in accepting the reality factor that there are limits to one's existence. How much more traumatic when loss of life is self-willed! Where do the survivors find consolation then? Suicide is the cruelest death of all for those who remain.

The "unpardonable sin" has been performed; the universal taboo with its theological imprimatur has been degradingly violated. Some say piously: "Suicide is self-murder. It is against the Sixth Commandment and the worst crime of all." Inwardly they hold the family and close friends partially or wholly accountable for the transgression.

For the relatives and friends, intolerable feelings of guilt and grief are aroused. The widowed spouse will never know if some act of unkindness on his or her part was the spark that inflamed the mate with the urge for self-execution. Parents feel that they must have failed their child miserably and blame themselves for the negligence. And the children of a suicide go through life haunted by the fact that they perhaps did something to expedite the parent's death. They may even believe that the cruel seed of self-destruction that destroyed their mother or father is lurking in themselves as well, that something is wrong with their psychological inheritance. There is the persistent, gnawing question,

"What did I do wrong?"

Survivors carry the stigma for life. Years afterward, a woman is still remembered as "the one whose husband shot himself." Suicide is never completely forgotten and forgiven.

110

But someone has died and must be buried. No matter how difficult the situation, there are still ways to be
of assistance to those who face the greatest tragedy and
challenge of their lives.

The Funeral
It is understandable that when the survivors hear
the shocking news their first impulse is to hold the funeral
as quickly and quietly as possible. After all, there is an
aura of shame and dishonor. As a result a private service is contemplated for the immediate family.

No matter how great the humiliation the relatives
just cannot hide from reality. Nor can one run away from
pain. A private funeral seems to say that the family is
unable to bear the disgrace before their friends and neigh-
bors and therefore want to keep it "secret." The family
overlook one important fact—that when given the opportunity, friends may be of help with supportive love.

The funeral offers an important opportunity to comfort the mourners. It is the rite of separation. The "bad
dream" is real. The presence of the corpse actualizes
the experience. In this way, the process of denial can be
transformed to the acceptance of reality.

In the eulogy, the clergyman should avoid any reference to blasphemy. The man who took his life was still a
man, with strengths as well as weaknesses. The positive
aspects of his life should be mentioned so that people can
recall the happy times with him and the many ways in
which life was enriched by his presence. After all, one
judges a person by his total years, and not by an isolated
moment, momentous as it may be.

111

Coming to Grips with Grief

The goals in ministering to the family of the suicide are similar to those in helping all who face bereavement. In Erich Lindemann's words:

"Grief work is emancipation from the bondage to the deceased, readjustment to the environment in which the deceased is missing, and the formation of new relationships."

But in comforting the bereaved, one must take into account the special kind of death. What can friends bring? Their best self—neither prejudiced by outmoded prohibitions, nor judgmental of the actions of the deceased or the survivors. They have not come either to justify or to censure; they have come, with love undiminished, as friends.

Conversation should be natural. Interest should be genuine and sincere. One should not try too hard. Over-solicitation only engenders further suspicions and guilt reactions. A most important method of encouraging grief work is by responsive listening and empathetic discernment to what the other experiences from his internal, agonizing frame of reference.

The survivor is often obsessed by the thought that he should have prevented the death, and sees himself a failure in the role of intervener. The guilt may take the form of self-recrimination, depression, and hostility. A tendency is to look for a scapegoat, often one who is least able to bear the added burden. There may be a direct charge: "You killed him! You allowed it to happen!" Inwardly the indictor may accuse himself, but he turns the anger outward in the attempt to cope with his own guilt. Minor omissions come to mind and loom as major, significant causes of death. Again and again, the survivor replays the ninth inning, devising those plays that might have won the game and preserved the life.

It is of no help to say: "Don't talk about it." The bereaved is going through an intense emotional crisis. He needs to articulate and act out his reactions—loud denial, turning slowly to bewilderment, and finally to the weeping, despairing confrontation with the truth of his loss.

Especially in a case of suicide the bereaved needs to pour out his heart. And what Sigmund Freud calls the "ties of dissolution" are so vital and therapeutic, that is, the sharing with the survivor of both pleasant and unpleasant memories of the deceased. When each event is reviewed, a pang is felt at the thought that the experience will never again be repeated. As pain is felt, the individual begins to slowly dissolve himself of his emotional ties to the dead person. A gradual working over of such old thoughts and feelings is a necessary part of the mourning process, and a prelude to the acceptance of the suicidal death as a real fact.

The survivor may believe that he was cast in the same mold as the suicide victim. He constantly recalls similarities, how they resembled one another both physically and mentally. He may begin to worry: "I keep thinking that I am losing my mind. I may kill myself someday. My father did, and I am just like him."

Since suicide is a blow and an affront to humanity, we repeatedly try to defend ourselves by saying that the suicidal person was out of his mind. But to inform a grieving individual that his loved one was "crazy" does not lighten the burden. Nor is it the truth. To quote Schneidman, Farberow, and Litman: "The majority of persons who commit suicide are tormented and ambivalent; they may be neurotic or have a character disorder, but they are not insane." Telling the survivors that the person was crazy does not add to their social status; it only brings the fear of inherited mental disease.

One might say: "There is much we do not know about suicide but we do know there is a limit to a load any person can bear. At that moment, death appeared the only alternative to his troubled life. But the ways of those closest to us are not necessarily our own ways." The professional and the friend can give an assurance which is predicated upon empirical studies: "This I can tell you: suicide is not inherited."

Pathological Grief

Among the many factors that can cause a distorted mourning reaction is an untimely loss by suicide. A death for which one is so completely unprepared has a more devastating impact than the loss of life from a

114

chronic disease. And self-execution can cause the survivor the greatest degree of torment, self-blame, and even mental illness.

When the grief work is not done, the survivor may suffer morbid distress characterized by delayed and pathological reactions. He may show great fortitude at the funeral but later develop symptoms of agitated depression and bodily affliction. He may complain of such psychosomatic diseases as ulcerative colitis, rheumatoid arthritis, asthma, and hypochondriasis (imaginary ills). Symptoms of a tension headache may lead to the conclusion by the bereaved that he has a brain tumor; arthritic pain is interpreted as heart disease; constipation becomes a symptom of a malignancy. Obsessive-compulsive behavior may manifest itself. He may try to appease his guilt through extreme cleanliness, or he may be unwilling to terminate the atmosphere of the funeral service, i.e., "Tell me the eulogy again." There may be self-destructive behavior detrimental to his social and economic existence.

In general, one is able to distinguish normal from pathological grief not by the latter's being abnormal or unusual per se, but rather by the reaction's being so intensive and prolonged that it, in turn, jeopardizes the physical and mental well-being of the person. If there are any doubts as to one's emotional health, professional help should be consulted. The period immediately following a suicidal death is a very precarious one, in which repressed wishes, forgotten memories, and contradictory thoughts can run riot under the stress of shock.

115

Withdrawal and Return

Following the suicidal death, the family often say:

"I would like to **escape** and
never come back." Some remain in the same home but
have run away as effectively as if they had moved to a
distant country. They withdraw into their own room,
isolate themselves from their friends and environment,
and dwell bitterly on their tormented state.

Their refuge may be self-medication, using either
alcoholic beverages or prescription drugs. The bereaved
may feel that sedatives and hypnotics which had been pre-
scribed for the now deceased or for themselves for a prior
malady must be safe or else the physician would not have
recommended it in the first place. Unfortunately, such a
solution may alleviate an anguished hour or a sleepless
night, but it leads to further withdrawal, loneliness, and
even addiction.

Some, in the desperate search for distraction at any
cost, become involved in the flight into activity. This
may involve a fanatic dedication to some political movement or a continuous round of breakfast, luncheon, cock-
tail, and dinner meetings, with successive telephone conversations of endless length in the interim. This is but a
temporary release of tension. The effort becomes abortive, for the bereaved soon grow weary from physical
fatigue and disenchanted with pseudo-involvements.

Said Edna St. Vincent Millay:

116

"Life goes on . .
I forget just why.

After the funeral, the survivor should take t
through which activities can bring him some
purpose. He should start slowly and move
this direction, with friends who are support
standing. Self-recrimination may still be p
the most meaningful way to relieve this guil
forming any errors of the past into a loving
more noble behavior in the future. His goa
late the grief experience and grow because
it.

In Hebrew there is a word T'shuva.
return," and implies the opportunity of a r
a fresh start, an ever new beginning. Pas
not doom a person forever. The willingne
temple of tomorrow's dreams on the grav
bitterness is the greatest evidence of the
spirit that fires the soul of man.

117

CHAPTER EIGHT

-- A Summons for Community Action

Making Death Come Alive

The new four-letter word of pornography is

DEAD.
Much of America
seems involved in a vast conspiracy to hush up this
"obscene" utterance. Like a noxious disease, death has
become a forbidden subject, replacing sex as an object
for repression.

Many not only avoid the word DEAD, they just pretend that loss of life does not occur. The anthropologist
Dr. Geoffrey Gorer states that forty-four percent of parents do not even tell their children when someone dies in
the immediate family! The same adults talk openly with
their offspring about the biological processes surrounding
the beginning of existence. However, they strangely avoid
the evidences of the end of the life cycle.

Death is disguised through euphemistic language.
People do not die. They "pass on." They "leave you."
They "go away on a long journey." Such fictions cater to
misconception and fantasy. When the finality of death is

121

replaced by the denial of reality, then the therapeutic mourning process is delayed and distorted.

This deception is practiced not only in a family where a death has occurred, but on a living patient as well. When a person is dying, the whole community enters into a secret alliance to keep the painful, but nevertheless real, fact from him. It little matters whether or not the individual wants the truth; he is not given it. So he is set apart because there is no honest communication. When one cannot talk about the most crucial thing in one's life, one cannot talk about anything else. Leo Tolstoy described this situation most poignantly in his novella The Death of Ivan Ilyich: "In the bosom of his family, surrounded by his friends, he was more alone than if he had been at the bottom of the sea, or the other side of the moon."

The universal fear of death in the United States extends to hospital personnel: physicians, nurses, and orderlies. Says Dr. Elizabeth K. Ross of the University of Chicago: "We often fail to see the dying patient as an ordinary human being, one who has great emotional needs as well as physical ones." She tells how she timidly approached a person who was dying of an incurable disease.

"He was so angry that he displaced it onto everyone. The nurses hated to go near him. But he wanted to talk,

and as soon as he began to
express himself, I found out
why he was angry. He had
so much to say and no one
had been willing to really sit
down and listen. "

No longer can the topic of death be avoided or
evaded. Mental health is not the denial of pain but the
frank acknowledgment of it. The world of biology is the
world of the living and dying. There can be no death
without life and, conversely, no life without death. Emo-
tion is natural, inevitable, and highly desirable. Grief
is more than sorrow. It is a necessary process that
forces a person to adjust to changed circumstances.
Even though no mortal has pierced the mystery of surrounding death, maturity should force man to recognize
that dying and death are phases of life and living.

Making Suicide More Understandable

Just as natural death cannot be ignored, neither can
self-imposed death. Suicide has been known in all times
and committed by all manner of people, from Saul, Sappho,
and Seneca to Virginia Woolf, James Forrestal, and
Marilyn Monroe. Attempted self-destruction, whether
completed or not, involves emotional turmoil, social

123

discord, and terrifying disruption of life. No task demands so much skill, understanding, empathy, and support as ministering to those downcast people who can no longer find purpose in life, or to the family who has experienced the loss of a loved one through self-inflicted death.

Dr. Karl Menninger states: "To the normal person, suicide seems too dreadful and senseless to be conceivable. There almost seems to be a taboo on the serious discussion of it. There has never been a wide campaign against it, as there has been against less easily preventable forms of death. There is no organized public interest in it. . . . In many instances, it could have been prevented by some of the rest of us."

Public Interest and Information

Dr. Menninger's campaign could be launched with a massive educational drive. The general population should be made aware of the clues to suicidal danger. The research of the social scientist should be translated into understandable and meaningful terms to enlighten the misinformed. There are some people who still believe that the whole subject is profane and should not be discussed. To them suicide is a declaration of guilt and sinfulness, or of an inability to endure physical or emotional pain, or it is a sign of poor moral fiber, or a demonstration of being just plain crazy. All must learn that no one is immune, that suicide appears in all ages, in both sexes, and on every economic level.

Mythologies must be unmasked. Even some professionals believe in the old bromide "Suicide comes

124

without warning. " This erroneous belief must be eradicated once and for all. The suicidal person often gives many indications of his intentions, if only the helper would listen.

People should know that those who attempt suicide must be given immediate assistance. Contrary to public opinion, the suicidal try is more than just an empty and dramatic act. Generally, matters get worse. After an escalation of longstanding problems and loss of meaningful relations, some people may well conclude that death is the only solution to unsolvable, unbearable, and chronic difficulties.

Also, every suicidal threat, whether articulated or disguised, must be taken seriously. Specific stressful situations, i. e. , death of a loved one, physical illness, economic distress, and domestic difficulties, may be conducive to self-inflicted death. Psychic and somatic signs of depression, indications of hysterical, psychopathic, and schizophrenic conditions, a history of past and present losses are other emotional precursors.

Just as the public has been alerted to the signs of cancer and heart disease, so would a program of information help the population become aware of the

danger signals

of suicide. And with equal benefit.

Special Training for "Gatekeepers"

The educational process must be extended to the "gatekeepers"—the physician, nurse, social worker, clergyman, and others who are most likely to hear hints that a person may take his life. Many of these people have the unique opportunity of being in a strategic position to identify and improve the potentially dangerous situation.

Psychological autopsies reveal that before the desperate act of self-execution, seventy-five percent of suicide victims had consulted their family physician, seventeen percent had visited a psychiatrist, seven percent had sought help from a social agency, and two percent had taken counsel with either a rabbi, minister, or priest.

Since the vast majority of patients had had a recent check-up with their doctor, the family physician is of central importance in suicide treatment and reduction. His influence is often greater than he himself realizes or sometimes desires. Unfortunately, this responsibility has not been fully met either by medical educators or practitioners.

For suicide is an anxiety-provoking subject which the physician, like everyone else, tends to avoid. The entire topic may arouse his own unresolved emotional disturbances and, therefore, interfere with his diagnosis and treatment of the patient. He fails to establish a meaningful relationship with the distraught person. The doctor often complains that he just does not have time to spend eliciting the agitated individual's underlying difficulties. After all, the waiting room is full. Yet, many physicians are hampered not only by an insufficiency of time but a lack of knowledge. They simply do not receive

126

an adequate training in the recognition and management of those bent on self-destruction.

In order to help the "gatekeepers," the study of the theory and prevention of suicide could become an integral part of the curriculum of medical, nursing, and theological schools. Not only would the professionals have some knowledge of the derivatives of emotional and interpersonal disturbances but they might also receive instruction in interviewing and counseling so they could relate more effectively to the real needs of the suicidal person and his family. They should learn the techniques of referral and the community resources that are available. Students might supplement their theoretical understanding with actual participation in suicide prevention centers. Such training would ensure the development of a cadre of understanding people who could later recognize suicidal threats, and thereby prevent the loss of precious life.

A Better Understanding for All

Instruction should be introduced on all levels — graduate and undergraduate, parental, in religious and public schools, in adult education classes. As a matter of fact, the largest registration ever recorded for a non-credit course sponsored by Wayne State University, University of Michigan, and Eastern Michigan State was for a course entitled, "Psychological Studies of Dying, Death, and Lethal Behavior." Such interdisciplinary aspects were discussed as: Violent and unnecessary deaths — can we prevent them? The experience of dying — what can we know about it?

In July, 1969, the University of Minnesota gave its

approval to the Department of Sociology for a Center for Thanatological Studies. The center's primary concern is with issues and problems connected with mortality in contemporary society. Original research is made into the subject of grief and bereavement; attitudes and responses to death and dying are studied.

Included in the curriculum are courses on suicide offered by those who have the greatest expertise in the field—the staff of the Minnesota Suicide Prevention Center. In Los Angeles, training programs are provided for college students, community mental health personnel, hospital staff, medical examiners, school counselors, lawyers, police, probation officers, clergy, and nonprofessional volunteers. In addition, there are postdoctoral fellowships in suicidology, for a period of three months.

There need not be special classes for the subjects of death and lethal behavior to be discussed. Health science students could profit by interviewing a dying patient. For the philosophy class, new insights would be afforded if the young people might have a dialogue with a chronically depressed suicide attempter.

Especially for the young, the time to discuss death is not when separation has taken place but when the children first broach the subject. In trying to help the youngster view death as an inevitable human experience, parents may in the process diminish their own bewilderment and distress. For the adults' real challenge is not how to explain death to their offspring but how to make peace with it themselves.

More Research

The most comprehensive listing of the world's material on suicide has recently been published by the U.S. Public Health Services National Institute of Mental Health. Containing more than 3,300 citations, the Bibliography on Suicide and Suicide Prevention lists articles and books dealing with every aspect of suicide—incidence, causes, treatment, and reduction.

Interestingly enough, the bibliography for the sixty years 1897–1957 contains only 1,200 items—one-third the number of references for the ten-year period 1957–1967. Suicide studies, which began during the earlier part of this century, have dramatically increased in the last decade.

A pioneering effort is the five-year, $852,000 grant from the National Institute of Mental Health to Johns Hopkins University for a fellowship in the study of suicide and its prevention. Says the director, Dr. Seymour Perlin: "It has been an extraordinarily successful program so far. We see ourselves as a national training center."

Despite these efforts, too little research has been attempted. Much of the accumulated material is anecdotal, or the result of independent clinical observation, or the product of investigation that has been inadequately controlled. Current treatment techniques are also in need of rigorous examination. For example, how effective is individual psychotherapy, pastoral counseling, drug prescription, or the community mental health program? And how accurate is the reporting of attempted and completed suicides? We have, at best, "guesstimates".

129

of how many acts of self-destruction occur annually. The reported numbers vary in reliability, depending on the community, the medical examiner, and the coroner. Only standardized measurements and persistent research can provide reliable baselines.

Unfortunately, the money that is so desperately needed for this lifesaving exploration has been siphoned off to war and defense. Billions of dollars are available for a voyage to the moon but pennies are offered for vital research and investigation. Especially needed are in-depth studies of the two groups most susceptible to suicide—the youth and the elderly.

Preventing Adolescent Suicide

Suicide among the youth is so horrifying and unthinkable to adults that many parents are complacent about the troubles of the young. To the older generation, Romeo and Juliet is a romantic and innocuous story. Yet, many adolescents cling to one another in similar love and

desperation. A modern Juliet
is likely to be
a frightened and
pregnant young lady;

the contemporary Romeo is an adolescent who feels rejected and thwarted. Both feel totally alone and forsaken.

When asked to whom they would turn if in trouble, over twenty-five percent of the youth responded that there

was no one who really cared or would understand them.
In a survey by Dr. Joseph D. Teicher, School of Medicine,
University of Southern California: "Of the forty-six percent who reported their intention to commit suicide to
other people, less than half shared the information with
their parents. Almost two-thirds of them talked to people
other than family members. This is particularly significant since

eighty-eight percent of the suicides occurred at home, very often with the parents in the next room!"

In every instance, the lack of communication between parent and child was a significant factor in the period preced-
ing the suicide.

It becomes obvious that there is much that can be
done to bring about a better relationship between adult and
youth. Breakdown frequently occurs when parents substitute their authority for honest answers to their offspring's
questions. Adults could spend more time listening to
their teen-agers and trying to comprehend what they are
really saying and thinking. The youth also have a responsibility to understand the adult's set of values. But both
adolescent and parent need not agree on all issues in order to communicate with each other. They can demonstrate in word and touch that even though there are differences, there is still love.

131

When serious problems arise, a professional should be consulted. Especially in colleges, comprehensive counseling services are desperately needed to assist the students in resolving the internal as well as the external struggles that complicate their lives.

If suicide is attempted, Dr. Teicher recommends that the youth be hospitalized, if only briefly, and placed in a ward where other adolescent patients might offer warmth, support, and understanding. For when the young people are first brought to the hospital they are shaken, anxious, insecure, depressed, guilty, and apprehensive because of the grief and anger that they have caused. The therapist can help them to understand the precipitating events, such as their parents' refusal to let them go out, or a broken romance, or a feeling that no one cares. He guides them to cope better with their conflicts and to communicate more effectively with their family and peers. He offers support in order that they might not feel so lonely and isolated. He should maintain contact from the beginning of the first consultation until the final rehabilitation or referral.

Preventing Suicide Among the Elderly

Although they make up only nine percent of the population, men and women over sixty-five years of age commit twenty-five percent of reported suicides. Were partial or installment-plan suicides included, the rates would be much higher. Elderly persons have their own ways of precipitating death before its natural time, by self-starvation, refusal to follow physicians' prescriptions, hazardous activity, and voluntary seclusion.

Among warning signs that a person may be contemplating an act of self-destruction are previous suicidal behavior, psychiatric disorders, the putting of his effects in order (although this may be merely appropriate behavior and must be so evaluated in the light of other events), and threats of suicide. The final cause may be a crisis, often "egoistic," during which the elderly person who lives outside of a group is deprived of the community's emotional support; such a crisis may be the death of close friends and relatives, loss of employment, economic insecurity, and feelings of rejection and uselessness.

Serious physical sickness is a most significant contributory factor. Many elderly persons appear to prefer death by their own hand rather than wait for it passively. In one study, it was found that eighty-five percent of the aged people who committed suicide had an active serious illness.

Admittedly, treatment of a depressed elderly individual is difficult. Not only may he have lost confidence in his own ability to cope with his problems, but he may believe (and often he is correct) that no one is really interested in him. The first step in turning such a person back to life is to establish trust. A sincere and decisive manner on the part of the helper will reassure even the confused individual that someone knows what must be done and will do it. Medical and psychotherapeutic support could be enlisted to ascertain both the physical and the psychological implications. A church or social agency might be contacted to determine the community's recreational and social resources for its senior citizens.

Other persons, particularly friends, colleagues,

133

and relatives, could be notified of the seriousness of the situation. The possibility of suicide should never be concealed or disguised. Hopefully, the significant others may comfort and assist the troubled person so that he may feel again the support of social ties.

A buddy system of calls and visits, and the use of aged persons at suicide prevention centers to answer the telephone and speak on the temptations to suicide, may be helpful. Many of these elderly have considered a self-inflicted death at one time or another and have much to offer the potential suicide.

Community Service Planning

Perhaps the most significant opportunity for the reduction of suicide is the creation and support of community mental health centers. This is a most meaningful way of meeting the real needs of a group through the development of facilities and staff into a comprehensive network of services. As the pressures of life increase and become more complicated, the sense of community becomes all the more urgent in establishing an effective program of mental health.

The community mental health center program is a comparatively new one. Its concepts are not completely tested or always appreciated even within the professional field. Nor are the roles of the staff of psychiatrist, psychologist, social worker adequately clarified and understood. In many aspects, it is still a vision, a dream yet to be fulfilled.

This revolutionary approach requires innovative, imaginative, and creative ideas. If it is to succeed in its

ultimate objectives, the program must first grow out of
and respond to the unique needs of the particular community. The center should reach out to all the people by
providing the greatest possible availability and accessi-
bility of help.

The bold new venture is in harmony with a relatively
recent orientation:

"preventive psychiatry."

This includes the inauguration of programs that emphasize
early treatment, rehabilitation, alternatives to hospitalization, strengthening the pattern of adaptation, and other
measures to prevent chronicity. By the early detection
of mental disorders and crisis situations, the incidence
of suicide can be drastically reduced.

A most important community facility for both prevention and intervention is the suicide prevention center.
The organization may be organized to operate autono-
mously or as part of an emergency hospital, local university, or mental health clinic. However structured, the
suicide prevention center should become part of the community's comprehensive mental health facilities.

Not only professionals but everyone can assist in
this endeavor. Some can play an important part in the
planning that must be done before, during, and after the
establishment of the center. Others can assist not only
philosophically but practically, by helping to raise funds
through individuals, private philanthropies, local govern-
ments, and federal aid programs. Proper personnel
should be employed to ensure a helping continuum for the
troubled person in the community. Carefully selected

135

volunteers have to be recruited and trained. In short, the suicide prevention center must be thoughtfully created, properly administered, and generously supported in order to extend maximum understanding and assistance.

A caretaker community is a caring community. It is bound together through pulsating relationships. The purpose is to open new vistas, stimulate constructive change, and convey an honest desire to promote health and wholeness. For self-imposed death is a complex problem in our society. But the caring individual and

community can do much to sustain **life.**

CHAPTER NINE

-- Epilogue

Life and death come into the world together; the eyes and the sockets which hold them are created at the same moment. From the moment I am born I am old enough to die. Life and death are contained within each other, complete each other, and are understandable in terms of each other. How to <u>die</u> means nothing less than how to <u>live</u>.

Going into the question of suicide means breaking open taboos. Suicide puts society, religion, and the community of souls <u>in extremis</u>. Self-destruction is the paradigm of the individual's independence from everyone else. This is the reason the law labels it "criminal" and religion has called it "sin."

But name-calling is of little avail. What is important is to understand those who cry for help, and support them in their hour of need in the most meaningful and constructive way.

There is something that all can bring to the moment of crisis. It is alluded to most poignantly in Thornton Wilder's <u>The Bridge of San Luis Rey</u>, when the bridge collapses and plunges the persons crossing it to their deaths. In the attempt to discover what it was in each

139

person's life that brought him to the ill-fated bridge of
self-destruction, Wilder enunciated one certain truth:
"There is a land of the living and a land of the dead and
the bridge is love—the only survival, the only meaning."

For it is
the death of love
that evokes
the love of death.

BIBLIOGRAPHY AND
SUGGESTED READINGS

Bibliography and Suggested Readings

Bibliography on Suicide and Suicide Prevention. 1897–
    1957, 1958–1967. Chevy Chase: National Institute
    of Mental Health, 1969.

Blaine, Graham B., Jr. Youth and the Hazards of Afflu-
    ence. New York: Harper and Row, 1966.

Choron, J. Death and Western Thought. New York:
    Collier Books, 1963.

Cohn, Edmond. The Moral Decision. Bloomington:
    Indiana University Press, 1955.

Douglas, Jack D. The Social Meanings of Suicide.
    Princeton, N.J.: Princeton University Press, 1967.

Dublin, Louis. Suicide: A Sociological and Statistical
    Study. New York: Ronald Press, 1963.

Durkheim, Emile. Suicide, A Study in Sociology.
    Glencoe, Ill.: Free Press, 1951.

Ellis, E. R. and G. N. Allen. Within Our Suicide
    Problem. New York: Doubleday, 1961.

Farber, Maurice L. Theory of Suicide. New York:
    Funk and Wagnalls, 1968.

Farberow, N. L. and E. S. Schneidman (Eds.). The Cry
    for Help. New York: McGraw-Hill, 1961.

Feifel, H. (Ed.). The Meaning of Death. New York:
    McGraw-Hill, 1961.

Fort, Joel. Suicide and the Special Problem of Being
    Young. San Francisco, October 15, 1967.

Freud, Sigmund. Civilization and Its Discontents. New
    York: W. W. Norton, 1962.
    _____. "Mourning and Melancholia," in Collected Papers,
    Vol. IV. London: The Hogarth Press, 1949.

Gibbs, J. P. Suicide. New York: Harper and Row, 1968.

Grollman, Earl A. "Pastoral Counseling of the Potential
    Suicidal Person," Pastoral Psychology, January,
    1966.

_____. _Rabbinical Counseling_. New York: Block, 1966.

Havens, Leston L. "Recognition of Suicidal Risks
Through the Psychological Examination," _New
England Journal of Medicine_, 276:210, 1967.

Hendin, Herbert. _Suicide and Scandinavia_. New York:
Grune and Stratton, 1964.

Henry, Andrew F. and James F. Short, Jr. _Suicide and
Homicide_. Glencoe, Ill.: Free Press, 1954.

Herzog, Arthur. "Suicide Can't Be Eliminated," _New
York Times Magazine_, March 20, 1966.

Hillman, James. _Suicide and the Soul_. New York:
Harper and Row, 1964.

Johnson, Paul. _Psychology of Pastoral Care_. New York
and Nashville: Abingdon Press, 1953.

Jung, Carl. _Modern Man in Search of a Soul_. New York:
Harcourt, Brace, 1933.

Liebman, Joshua L. _Peace of Mind_. New York: Simon
and Schuster, 1946.

Lindemann, Eric and Ina M. Greer. "A Study of Grief:
Emotional Responses to Suicide," _Pastoral
Psychology_, December, 1953.

Meerloo, Joost A. M. _Suicide and Mass Suicide_. New
York: Grune and Stratton, 1962.

Menninger, Karl A. _Man Against Himself_. New York:
Harcourt, Brace, 1938.

Miller, Dorothy H. and Daniel Godman. "Predicting
Post-Release Risk Among Hospitalized Suicide
Attempters," _Omega_, February, 1970.

Murphy, Kenneth B. _Loneliness — The Surest Sign_.
Rescue, Inc.
_____. _Lost Scholars_. Rescue, Inc.
_____. _Suicide, An Attempt Problem_. Rescue, Inc.
_____. _Suicide, A Species of Felony_. Rescue, Inc.
_____. _The Tempestuous Storms_. Rescue, Inc.
_____. _The Vacant Seat_. Rescue, Inc.

Pretzel, Paul W. "The Role of the Clergyman in Suicide
Prevention," _Pastoral Psychology_, April, 1970.

144

Resnik, H. L. P. "Center Comments," <u>Bulletin of</u>
    <u>Suicidology</u>, National Institute of Mental Health,
    Spring, 1970.
_____ (Ed.). <u>The Diagnosis and Management of the Sui-</u>
    <u>cidal Individual</u>. Boston: Little, Brown and Com-
    pany, 1967.
_____ and Joel M. Cantor. "Suicide and Aging," <u>Journal</u>
    <u>of the American Geriatric Society</u>, February, 1970.

Richman, Joseph and Milton Rosenbaum. "The Family
    Doctor and the Suicidal Family," <u>Psychiatry in</u>
    <u>Medicine</u>, January, 1970.

St. John-Stevas, Norman. <u>Life, Death and the Law</u>.
    Bloomington: Indiana University Press, 1961.

Shneidman, E. S. (Ed.). <u>Essays in Self-Destruction</u>.
    New York: International Science Press, 1967.
_____ and N. L. Farberow. <u>Clues to Suicide</u>. New
    York: McGraw-Hill, 1957.
_____ and Philip Mandelkorn. <u>How to Prevent Suicide</u>.
    Public Affairs Pamphlet No. 406, 1967.

Seiden, Richard H. "Campus Tragedy: A Study of Student
    Suicide," <u>Journal of Abnormal Psychology</u>, 3:285-289,
    1966; and in <u>Contemporary Research in Personality</u>,
    2nd ed., edited by I. G. Sarason. Princeton: Van
    Nostrand, 1969.

Sprott, S. E. <u>The English Debate on Suicide</u>. LaSalle,
    Ill.: Open Court Publishing Company, 1961.

Stengel, Erwin. <u>Suicide and Attempted Suicide</u>.
    Baltimore: Penguin Books, 1964.

Teicher, Joseph D. "Why Adolescents Kill Themselves,"
    <u>National Health Program Reports</u>, January, 1970.

Williams, Glanville. <u>The Sanctity of Life</u>. New York:
    Knopf, 1957.